Texas Press

The Fair

By Juan José Arreola
Translated by John Upton
This wry and remarkable book by the noted Mexican satirist Arreola is unique in modern Latin American fiction. Although *The Fair* must be defined as a novel, it is in fact a variegated fabric of interwoven stories, vignettes, lamentations, sardonic observations, confessions, diatribes, documentary fragments, and still lifes.
Texas Pan American Series
162 pages, illustrated
$10.00

The Devil's Church and Other Stories

By Machado de Assis
Translated by Jack Schmitt and Lorie Ishimatsu
A master of the short story and an early experimenter in psychological realism, Machado launches a devastating satirical attack on society through his fiction. These nineteen stories are representative of Machado's innovative style and world view, and this translation doubles the number of his stories previously available in English.
165 pages, illustrated
$10.00

The Decapitated Chicken and Other Stories

By Horacio Quiroga
Selected and translated by Margaret Sayers Peden
The *New Yorker* noted that the tales in this haunting collection "are, like Poe's, full of psychological shocks and eerie effects, and are bracingly, if ruthlessly, realistic."
Texas Pan American Series
195 pages, illustrated
$8.95

The Siren & The Seashell and Other Essays on Poets and Poetry

By Octavio Paz
Translated by Lysander Kemp and Margaret Sayers Peden
Reflecting on individual poets and poetry in general, Paz makes each essay the occasion for a wider discussion of cultural, historical, psychological, and philosophical themes.
"Octavio Paz is a sinewy stylist and one of the strengths of his prose is to give concreteness to the virtually inexpressible."
—*The Boston Globe*
Texas Pan American Series
196 pages, illustrated
$9.95

University of Texas Press
Box 7819
Austin, Texas 78712

Review 77

Editor
Ronald Christ
Associate Editor
Rosario Santos
Assistant Editor
Gregory Kolovakos
Circulation
Pamela Zapata
Editorial Assistants
Donna Hildreth
Rita Kohn

Advisory Board
Anna Balakian
José Guillermo Castillo
Zunilda Gertel
Victoria Ocampo
José Miguel Oviedo

**Cover: Manuel Felguérez. "Selección de un círculo," 1975.
Enamel on canvas, 49″ x 59″**

Review is published three times a year by the Center for Inter-American Relations. The Center, a non-profit, membership corporation financed by foundation support, membership dues and corporate as well as individual gifts, conducts educational programs in the visual and performing arts, literature and public affairs. Subscription rates for Review: $5.00 yearly within the United States; $6.25 foreign; $8.00 institutions. Past issues available. All subscriptions should be addressed to Review, Center for Inter-American Relations, 680 Park Avenue, New York, N.Y. 10021. Unsolicited manuscripts in English are welcome but will not be returned unless accompanied by a stamped, self-addressed envelope. All translations must be accompanied by the original Spanish or Portuguese. Neither the editors nor the Center can be responsible for damage or loss of such manuscripts. Opinions expressed by Review are those of the individual writers and not necessarily of the editors or the Center. Copyright © 1976 by the Center for Inter-American Relations, Inc. Library of Congress Cat. No, 74-86354. All rights reserved. Microfilms of issues 1- 19 available from University Microfilms, Inc., 300 N. Zeeb Road, Ann Arbor, Mich. 48106.

Manuel Felguérez

On any list of important contemporary Latin
American artists, the name of Manuel Felguérez is
sure to figure. But Felguérez's achievement is not
merely an individual one. As Octavio Paz explains,
Felguérez belongs to a historical development in art
as well:
"Between 1950 and 1960 the generation to which
Felguérez belongs—Cuevas, Rojo, Gironella, Lilia
Carrillo, García Ponce—undertook a task of
esthetic and intellectual hygiene: the cleansing of
minds and canvases. These were young people with
vast appetites, limitless curiosity and sound
instincts. Surrounded by general incomprehension,
but determined to re-establish the universal flow of
ideas and forms, they were doing enough to open
the windows. Air from the outside world diffused
into Mexico. Thanks to them our young artists can
breathe a little better now."*
Subsequently, Felguérez developed what Paz calls
"relief polychromes," which led to experiments in
creating through duplicating, which in turn led to
extraordinarily innovative experiments involving
the use of a computer.
In the following FOCUS, we offer an opportunity to
trace the development of this artist through his own
words and through those of his fellow innovator,
the well-known novelist Juan García Ponce. Tracing
this development, you will witness the evolution of
a major artist whose esthetic successes originate in
a rare lucidity and issue in an even rarer sensuous
pleasure.

*Octavio Paz, "Multiple Space," translated by Rachel Phillips in Manuel
Felguérez's Paintings and Sculpture, Carpenter Center for the Visual Arts,
Harvard University, December, 1976.

Chronology

MANUEL FELGUEREZ

1928 On December 12, Manuel Felguérez is born at the San Agustín Ranch, Valparaíso, Zacatecas, to Manuel Felguérez Ramírez and Consuelo Barra Aspe. The family moves to Mexico City when Felguérez is seven and his father's death decides their permanent residence in that city. Felguérez carries out his studies in Marist schools: primary and secondary school at the Colegio México, preparatory school at Francés Morelos. During those years, he belongs to the Boy Scouts and in 1947, after attending an international jamboree in France, he travels through Europe and decides to become a painter. Upon his return to Mexico, however, he enrolls in the School of Medicine and the Academy of San Carlos, abandoning the first after a month, the second after six.

He studies archaeology. With Jorge Wilmont he hikes through the country searching for pre-Columbian pieces so he can sell them and return to Europe. The undertaking fails, but Felguérez nevertheless starts out, in a series of "pushes," first to New York and from there, working on a boat, to Sweden, then through the Scandinavian countries, Germany, Belgium.

1950 He finally arrives in Paris and stays there for two years, working as a subject at the Psychology of Sensation Laboratory at the College de France, studying French civilization at the Sorbonne, taking a draw-ing course at the Louvre, giving lectures on Mexican muralism at workers' unions. Activity centered on the sculpture he creates in the workshop of Zadkine, whom he considers his true teacher. Frequents Brancusi's workshop in Montparnasse. Zadkine and Brancusi are the two sculptors who influence his initial work.

1953 Returns to Mexico and enters the workshop of Francisco Zúñiga with whom he works as an assistant on the frieze Zúñiga makes for the Veracruz lighthouse. Sells his first works at a gallery directed by Lola Alvarez Bravo. Attends the course in modern art Justino Fernández gives at the Faculty of Philosophy. Marries Ruth Rohde.

1954 His first daughter, Patricia, is born and the family moves to Puerto Escondido, Oaxaca. Using local clay and baking it in bread ovens, Felguérez prepares a series of terra cottas that he shows in his first one-man show at the French Institute of Latin America. As a result of this exhibition, he is given a scholarship by the French government.

1955 Returns to work with Zadkine in Paris and following his advice, works in a studio of the Casa de México where he participates in an exhibition-contest, receiving a prize for sculpture. Exhibits in the resident "Foreign Artists Show" at the Petit Palais.

1956 Programs in Art and Design are created at the Universidad Iberoamericana in Mexico, under the directorship of Matías Goeritz, who asks Felguérez to be an instructor in sculpture, a position he holds for five years. Exhibits work brought from Paris at the Carmel-Art Gallery. Second daughter Karina is born.

1957 Takes part in the group show with which the Antonio Souza Gallery is inaugurated in Mexico City, where he exhibits sculpture along with Lilia Carrillo, who shows painting. Participates in the Gulf Caribbean Art Exhibit at the Museum of Modern Art in Boston.

1958 First one-man exhibition of painting Antonio Souza Gallery. Shows at the National Gallery in the Palace of Fine Arts in Mexico City, the XX Biennial Exhibition of Watercolor at the Brooklyn Museum and the Martin Schwerg Gallery in St. Louis, Missouri. One of his sculptures is acquired by the Weiner Sculpture Collection of Fort Worth, Texas. Travels to New York and signs with the Bertha Shaffer Gallery, which presents his work as part of "Sculpture Selections" (1958 to 1959).

1959 Second show of painting at the Antonio Souza Gallery; the Museum of Modern Art in Mexico City acquires one of his works. Selected to participate in the "First Biennial Exhibition of Young Artists" in Paris. Completes his first sculptured mural —a multicolor relief of mosaic and marble —for an apartment building in Mexico City.

1960 Exhibits at the Panamerican Union, which acquires one of his works for its permanent collection. Marries Lilia Carrillo in Washington; they travel to New York and Felguérez exhibits painting at the Bertha Shaffer Gallery. Participates in the "Second Biennial Interamerican Exhibition" in Mexico and donates a work to the Bezabel Museum in Jerusalem. Creates his first stage set for *La dame aux Camelias*. Juan García Ponce writes his first critical essay on Felguérez's work. Participates with a group of young painters in a movement against the director of the National Institute of Fine Arts. The Museum of Contemporary Art is created as a result, with Miguel Salas Anzures named director. After the death of Salas Anzures, the project for a museum independent of the government is interrupted.

1961 Chosen to participate in the Second Biennial Exhibition of young painters in Paris as well as the Sixth Biennial in Tokyo. A special invitation to the Sixth Biennial Show of São Paulo makes possible the participation of a group of Mexican painters, independent of government support; travels to Brazil as the chief representative of this group. Creates the Iron Mural at the Diana Cinema, causing a great

debate. The work is launched with a Happening, directed by Alexandro Jodorowsky and attended by more than a thousand people, and suffers a series of attacks from the company controlling the cinema, which destroys the work's original setting and uses it for hanging posters and announcements. As member of the Theater of the Avant-Garde directed by Jodorowsky, creates sets for 20 works, among them: Strindberg's *Ghost Sonata* (closed after its opening), Jodorowsky's *Opera of Order* (closed during its run) and Ionesco's *The Lesson*. The Juan Martín Gallery is opened and Felguérez shows with this gallery from this date on.

1962 Travels to Peru where he exhibits in the Institute of Contemporary Art in Lima; travels throughout the country and gives a talk on new Mexican painting at the school of Fine Arts. Participates in the "First Biennial Exhibition of Sculpture" in Mexico and is given an award in the category of Integration with Architecture. Creates an "Ensemblage" of 96 industrial products for the Mexican Pavilion at the World's Fair in Seattle. The Museum of Modern Art in New York tries to acquire this work but Mexican authorities reject the offer, saying it belongs to the nation. From that time on the work is left in a warehouse belonging to the Department of Industry and Business. Designs the set for the Ballet Intramuros at the Palace of Fine Arts. Takes part in the short-lived work presented by the Theater of the Avant-Garde in the Villaurrutia Room of the School of Theater; this Happening is attacked by pseudo-religious organizations and ends in police intervention. Designs handicrafts and begins production of a sculpture series in terra cotta. Exhibits at the Juan Martín Gallery and participates in the "Contemporary Painting in Mexico" show at the National Museum of Uruguay.

1963 Exhibits in the Juan Martín Gallery and is selected for the "Contemporary Art of America and Spain" show in Madrid and Barcelona. From oyster and abalone shells as well as from mother-of-pearl, constructs the 500 square meter *Song to the Ocean*

"Olimpiada Mexico 68." Metal sculpture. 5 x 15 x 3 m.

Sculptured Environment, 1969. Steel, glass and iron.

Vitreous Sculpture, 1970 (Exterior). Metal, glass and automotive machinery. 4 x 12 m.

mural at a popular pool in the sports complex. This work is unveiled with a huge pageant based on Lautréamont's *Song to the Ocean*, directed by Jodorowsky and attended by more than three thousand people. Constructs a sculptured wall from discarded building materials that is shown at the Dynamic Museum—the Conceptual Museum is already gone—as an entry in the category of integrating plastic arts with public housing. Takes part in the Happening-Spectacle at the National School of Plastic Arts. The Industrial Club, directed by Jaime Saldívar, acquires a work of his for its permanent collection.

1964 Has a retrospective show at the Casa del Lago. Intense activity in creating works integrated with architecture: *The Destructive Invention*, a mural sculpture constructed from brass, pieces of polychromatic machinery and plastic threads for the Confederation of Industrial Boards; a metal curtain and a stained glass sculpture for the Teatro de la Paz; sculptured armor created from pieces of machinery for the Palacio Municipal of Nuevo Laredo. The authorities ordered the armor thrown into the river but, because of a strong publicity campaign, the order was not executed. In reprisal, however, Felguérez was not paid. Collaborates with the architect Ramírez Vázquez on the design of lattice work for the central patio of the National Museum of Anthropology. Travels to Nuevo Laredo with a group of painters to inaugurate the Martí Gallery and joins other artists in the production of the movie *Tajimara* by Juan José Gurrola.

1965 Presents a work in the show "Artistic Attitudes," a selection of contemporary Mexican and North American art chosen by Juan García Ponce and by Harold Rosenberg respectively at the Aristos Gallery. Participates in the "Esso Show" at the Museum of Modern Art in Mexico as well as in the scandal the show's inauguration caused. Exhibits in the Collection of Contemporary Mexican Paintings at the Casa de las Américas in Havana, and in the exhibition "Two Years of Painting" at the

Casa del Lago. Creates the series of sculptured murals entitled *Slavery in Egypt* for the David Maguen Synagogue.

1966 Shows at the Juan Martín Gallery. Travels to Havana to show his work at the Casa de las Américas, which acquires a work of his for its permanent collection. Forms part of the selection committee for "Confrontation 66"; participates in this exhibition as well as in "Mexican Painting of Today" at the Faculty of Chemical Sciences in Ciudad Universitaria. His sculpture is part of "Mexican Sculpture" (from all periods) that travels throughout Central and South America. Creates a concrete wall for the new Juan Martín Gallery. Participates in roundtables for "Modern Art of Mexico" at the School of Plastic Arts at the National University. Along with Octavio Paz, is a visiting teacher and critic at the School of Architecture, Cornell University, during the Latin American year held by that university.

1967 Participates in the symposium organized by the Inter-American Foundation for the Arts in Caracas, Venezuela. Collects work for the Mexican section of "Popular Art of America and Spain" at the Museum of the Americas in Madrid. Travels to Bogotá, Colombia for an exhibition initiating the series "The Future Eve" (inspired by the novel of V. de L'Isle Adam) at the University Museum of Modern Art, where he participates in a roundtable on Art and Architecture. That museum and the Library of the Banco de la República acquire works of his. Travels to Spain with Lilia Carrillo to collaborate on the mounting of "Popular Art of America and Spain." Initiates his geometric work with five sculptures in "Kalicosmia 67," an exhibition presented at the Museum of Modern Art in Mexico City and supported by the plastics industry. Creates a sculpture for the entrance to the Mexican Pavilion at Expo 67 in Montreal, Canada. Has a retrospective show at the Israeli Club and participates in the "Third National Show of Sculpture" at the Museum of Modern Art, Mexico City. Lectures at the Iberoamerican University on the artistic integration of sculpture and is juror for "New Values," an exposition organized at the Casa del Lago.

1968 Presents the last phase of the series "The Future Eve" at the Juan Martín Gallery. Participates in the "First Triennial Exhibition" in India, winning the second International Prize for painting. The Museum of Modern Art in New Delhi acquires one of his works. Travels to San Antonio, Texas, to create a snail shell mural for the exterior of the Mexican Pavilion in Hemisferia 68. Films a Happening for a short feature at the Mexican Olympics (not shown). Designs handcrafted figures of polychromatic metal. The Olympic Committee commissions a monument, later donated to the Museum of Modern Art where it can presently be found (incomplete). On account of the events surrounding the Olympics, refuses, along with several other artists, to participate in the Solar Salon, an official activity presented at the Fine Arts Museum at the same time as the Olympics. Initiates and participates in the founding of the Independent Salón. Elected a member of the co-ordinating board of the Committee of Artists and Intellectuals of the Student Movement of 1968. Collaborates with the School of Philosophy and Letters' *Comité de Lucha* in the organizing of a collective mural, created by a large number of painters at the statue of Miguel Alemán at the National University. This mural was destroyed during the military occupation of the University.

1969 Holds two one-man shows: at the Juan Martín Gallery and the Lepe de Puerto Vallarta Gallery. Participates in the show "Masterworks of Mexican Art" presented at the Palace of Fine Arts in Paris, as well as in the "Young Artists of the World" organized by the Play-Group, Inc., Foundation in New York. Chosen for the World Selection of 65 artists who participate in the exhibition "Dialogue Between the East and the West" inaugurating Tokyo's Museum of Modern Art, which acquires one of his works. Creates a collage of printing materials for the Madero Printing Co. Appointed teacher of formal design when the National University creates the School of Architecture and Design; holds that post for two years. Travels to Cuba to be a judge at an exhibition in Havana. Participates in round-tables on exhibitions and museums organized by the Independent Salón and the Casa del Lago. Builds a sculpture-environment for the CYDSA Company.

1970 Presents a grouping of geometric elements with optical effects at the Third Independent Salón at the National University's Museum of Arts and Sciences. Co-authors a collective mural at Expo 70 in Osaka, Japan. Joins the National School of Plastic Arts as a teacher, directing an experimental workshop. Serves on the commission developing the curriculum for the program of Visual Arts. Travels to Cuba to attend the symposium of Salón 70 and participates with LeParc, Matta and Saura in the development of the themes of that meeting. Named a judge in a poster competition organized by the National University's Museum of Arts and Sciences.

1971 Shows geometric work with reflecting, optical illusions at the Juan Martín Gallery. Participates in the final activity of the Independent Salón—creating one of the exterior murals for the Center of Contemporary Art in Guadalajara—before the Salon is closed by the collective resignation of the organization's principal members. After a competition, and on the basis of his merits, he is named head of visual research at the National School of Plastic Arts by agreement of the university council and is elected technical adviser to that school.

1972 Helps in the set-design for Alexandro Jodorowsky's movie *The Sacred Mountain*, making sculptures and a large number of other objects. Exhibits a work in the "Painters from Zacatecas" show at the former convent of San Agustín, Zacatecas. Works of his are acquired for the formation of the initial collections of the Museums of Modern Art of Toluca and Patzcuaro. Participates in the "Third Iberoamerican Exhibition" in Medellín, Colombia. Elected a member of the organizing committee for the

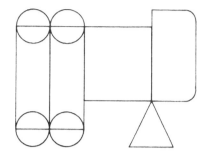

first national congress of plastic artists as well as of the editorial committee for the resolutions of that committee. Participates in the symposium on museums at the Museum of San Carlos. Travels to the United States as a guest of the Kansas National Sculpture Conference, organized by the University of Kansas. Named head of the College of Visual Education at the National School of Plastic Arts.

1973 Inducted into the Academy of Arts after being nominated by the Sculpture division. Participates in the Art-Technology show presented by the Mexican-North American Institute. Donates a work to the Museum of Solidarity with Chile (an action interrupted by the assassination of President Allende). Opens "The Multiple Space" show in December at the Museum of Modern Art in Mexico City which acquires a group of his works. Rufino Tamayo acquires a work for the museum he is forming.

1974 His wife Lilia Carrillo dies on June 6th. Exhibits graphic work at the Kaufmann Graphics Gallery in Houston, Texas, and in the House of Culture in Guadalajara. Participates in the selection of Mexican painting that travels to the Museums of Modern Art in Tokyo and Osaka. Co-chairperson of the first International Congress on Economy and Urban Development in the city of Guanajuato. Hired as a researcher by the Co-ordination of Humanities at the National University. Travels to Buenos Aires with a group to meet with Argentine intellectuals as a result of the Mexican president's visit to Argentina. Travels to Africa as a member of the Mexican mission organized by the Autonomous Metropolitan University to study Mexican technical assistance for the design of buildings and the integration of art in the construction of Dodoma, the new capital of Tanzania. Member of the Center of Artistic and Scientific Research. Leaves his teaching activities to devote himself full-time to research into the possibilities of cybernetics in the production of design for the Co-ordination of the Humanities. Wins a Guggenheim Fellowship.

1975 Wins the Grand Award of Honor in the XIII Biennial Exhibition of São Paulo, Brazil.

1976 Appointed research member of the Carpenter Center for the Visual Arts at Harvard University and participates in various conferences and roundtables at such institutions as the National University of Mexico, the Museum of Modern Art, the University of Veracruz. Publishes five articles, including "El Espacio Múltiple" in *Plural* and "La necesaria pluralidad del arte latinoamericano" in *Revista Artes Visuales*. Exhibits in five one-man shows—four in Mexico and one at Harvard—and takes part in four group shows, three in Mexico and one originating at the Palace of Fine Arts in Brussels that travels through Yugoslavia, Iran, and Luxembourg. ○

Making Spirit Matter

JUAN GARCIA PONCE
Translated by Gregory Kolovakos

Sometimes while tracing the evolution of an artist's entire work, we suddenly discover that it has grown, developed in the course of inevitable deviations, discoveries and failed experiments, like an organic entity of whose inevitable, inner unity—despite superficial, external differences—the artist himself may be unconscious. The works have their own autonomy, speak for themselves and it is those works, not the artist, that can best lead us back through their own reality to their origins, clarifying their meaning and enabling us to enjoy them more deeply.

Standing in front of Manuel Felguérez's mural in the offices of the Confederation of Industrial Boards, and now, once again, in front of his more recent works, I have found myself remembering the general appearance of his first studio, which I knew before I knew any of his works. It was many years ago. Maybe at that time Felguérez was only beginning to play with the idea of being a sculptor. Whatever shape it was in, the studio was not yet an artist's workshop, but only a room where Felguérez brought some objects together with others from which he liked to "make things." And the variety of those objects was what turned out to be fascinating. In that room Felguérez had rocks of all sorts, pieces of wood, twisted roots, bark from trees whose tex-

JUAN GARCIA PONCE, winner of the Villaurrutia Prize in 1972 for his collection of short stories, *Encuentros*, has published numerous volumes of critical essays and narrative prose.

ture appealed to him, fragments of plaster. He also tried to dissect animals there. Mostly, I think, with very little success, because there was a piercing odor of decomposition in the studio. But the important thing is that even though he occasionally tried to make something out of those objects by working with them, polishing them or covering them with plaster, they were there, first and foremost, because their forms attracted him, said something to him.

Much later, I saw one of the earliest exhibitions of Felguérez's sculpture in Mexico. He had travelled throughout Europe and spent a long time in Paris. Showing the influence of Henry Moore and of Zadkine, who had been his teacher, each new work leaned toward greater abstraction, tended to search further for simplification of form by eliminating superfluous details. But these works also revealed his continual search for an enveloping, circular form that would enclose the sculpture in itself, that in a certain manner would convert its space into a closed boundary. His treatment of materials revealed a trenchant sensitivity: the same capacity to rejoice in the value of textures, the hardness and permeability of stone or terra cotta.

Afterwards, Felguérez changed mediums and presented a huge and surprising exhibition of painting. He was already and unequivocally an abstract painter with a sure sense of composition. Done for the most part in red and gray tones organized as a set of small planes and inscribed within a more ample, total form that contained them, his paintings always achieved within their multiple variations an admirable unity of composition on the general plane of the canvas. They had, moreover, a richness of texture, of materials—sensuous, alive and delicate at the same time—accompanied by a splendid chromatic sense. In these paintings, Felguérez apparently succeeded in combining a sensory awareness of matter and an understanding of the flat space of the canvas with the mass of a sculpture's volumes and the sensuous power of colors. That exhibition immediately placed him among the most prominent young painters of Mexico.

At that time he had his studio on Tabasco Street. Instead of paintings on the walls, there was a collection of butterflies perfectly arranged in several display cases, and, on a piece of furniture, there stood out a small, iron and brass kettle whose function I was never able to understand, but which had all the beauty of an absurd and arbitrary *bibelot*. Felguérez had exclusively specialized in painting since his first exhibition, but now his canvases were very different, in a certain sense, from those he had shown there. Before he sent them to Washington, I had an opportunity to see in that studio the series of works he showed at the Panamerican Union in 1960. Without emerging from the strict abstractionism he had chosen ever since his beginning, the painter almost completely renounced the chromatic scale's emotive value that enriched his first paintings. With absolute austerity, his palette was limited to black and white—both elaborated to a particular richness and achieving an opacity available to all sorts of suggestions within their foremost treatment as mere surfaces voluntarily renouncing any sort of emphasis. The small planes and smudges had also disappeared, giving way to large surfaces, underscored by the careful treatment of textures. The conjunction of those white and black planes, which often seemed to oppose one another, revealed a sure power of composition and Felguérez always managed the balance, the unity of the planes miraculously. As a group, the paintings disclosed a rigor-

ous desire to liberate expressive power from matter itself, establishing a play of tensions within its apparent repose, its geometric, serious and weighty equilibrium. Space once again closed in on itself in a way different from the demands of the plane but still with the same internal purpose of creating a self-sufficient order that converts each painting into a pure object, a serene, luminous and self-ruling image essentially opposed to the external chaos. In this way, Felguérez's painting transcended the expressive possibilities of his formal means. The painter required color to stop being merely color; he subjected color to the demands of the material, so only the latter would speak in his works, revealing itself to us. In the same way, he simplified shapes to the maximum, so they would be only planes, only surfaces where texture was the one sensual element. Within their severity—their renunciation of adjectivization, of commentary—Felguérez's works nevertheless had the serious and profound power of painting itself.

The latent energy in those paintings broke the geometric balance that restrained energy in the later works of Felguérez. In his next exhibition, white was already the single color remaining in his most recent work; but stasis, the serene repose of the planes, had also disappeared, along with the search for textures and shapes enriching the earlier play of separation and integration among those planes. In their place, Felguérez gave his brush strokes free run, accentuating their instinctive quality so they would turn into the unique justification of the created forms, and only later did he seek the indispensable balance by consciously ordering and correcting the initial effect. Less sure, but freer and more lyrical at the same time, the works of that period indicate, in some way, the artist's return to the natural language of painting. The sign, the energy liberated by the painter's brush, gave way to the creation of a series of pure plastic rhythms, which came to take the place of the earlier volumetric mass. Thus, Felguérez's paintings became less sculptured. Little by little, they were renouncing his earlier objectivity in order to search out a more subjective, instinctive and emotional form of expression, but one that was always resolved in the creation of a strict, closed order within the totality of the composition. Along this line, it was natural for color to reappear in the subsequent paintings and to take the place of texture in the earlier works. With color, Felguérez accented the purely plastic character of his works even more. Red and blue—right out of the tube and applied directly in rapid, nervous brush strokes—created new planes, established a new play of forces, and transformed the initial insecurity into a perfectly balanced, internal tension.

Within the totality of Felguérez's work, not even one of these successive transformations can be seen as gratuitous, nor can any be considered merely formal experiments. The surprising unity of Felguérez's work demonstrates that without doubt the artist has continually tried to enrich his means of expression, but that he has done so with an absolute fidelity to his original vision. Each of his searches and discoveries obeys that ultimate need to achieve—with color or volume, on canvas or in stone—that perfection of form through which objects seem to suddenly acquire meaning and reveal to us a truth contained within them, represented by them. Therefore, in the works of Manuel Felguérez, experimentation is never merely formal, never a self-gratification, but rather, and above all else, a way of forcing his means of expression, of compelling them to go further, to transcend themselves in order to encounter form filled with natural meaning. And Felguérez has seen that meaning; he has intuited it previously in many other objects, perhaps even deciding to create them himself. For me, that original intuition explains to a large extent the nature of his work, its ultimate sense, and it brings us directly to an important facet of his work: the series of murals.

The facility with which Felguérez has moved in his work from sculpture to painting shows that he truly has never established any difference between the values that the two mediums seek to express. So it is natural that in his murals he has sought

a union of the two, attempting to add volume to the flat surface and finally eliciting relief. In this sense, Felguérez's murals contain solutions that in their accommodation to the plane, in the meaning of the forms, correspond to painting; but the murals are realized with the materials of sculpture and offer volume more than color. Nevertheless, the elements used in their realization allow us to suppose that the discovery in back of their creation dates from quite far back.

At the beginning of this essay I said that Felguérez's last mural reminded me of his old fondness for a series of objects whose form seemed to say something to him. I think this same fondness, this ability to find meaning in a series of objects owing its arrangement to chance or to a mere whim of nature, is the point of departure for these murals with which Felguérez has given a new dimension to his art. Kurt Schwitters declares that "provided only with blotting paper, every artist should be allowed to create a painting, always and only when he is able to create a painting with it." Among the stage sets that Manuel Felguérez has made for the theater as a marginal aspect of his work, but which nonetheless occupy a place within it, he included a sort of chair-machine for Ionesco's The Lesson that truly had its own value as sculpture. This object also reminded me of the small kettle he kept in his studio. Like that kettle, the chair-machine had a function—it was used within the play—but its form acquired an autonomous value, transcending that utilitarian function and transforming itself into an object of art capable of conferring value by itself. Still, in the creation of those stage sets, Felguérez has ironically played with various aspects of contemporary art, and the chair-machine in addition to the kettle in his studio, recalled Tingeley's sculptures, in the same way that other of Felguérez's stage sets ironically employed the formal devices of Schwitters or Burri. In the murals, that ironic play has disappeared. The will to transcend the original function of the objects persists, however, incorporating these objects into another reality and bestowing on them a distinct value that is independent of their real essence but making use of their capacity to suggest formal elements.

Thus, Felguérez created his first mural with scrap metal, and in the following ones he has successively used oyster shells, remnants of industrial products, fragments of construction materials, brass and handicrafts, old machinery iron, brass and plastic threads, and old iron and glass. On some occasions the nature of the materials has been forced upon him; on all, the means of using them is the same. Felguérez has directly incorporated those materials into his work, has let them be what makes the work possible, let them be the work itself; but he has done so with full consciousness that if it is possible to make a painting with blotting paper, this can only be successfully achieved by making the blotting paper transcend its own nature. In this sense, his procedure moves away from the inclusive technique of collage. He does not try to incorporate foreign objects into his works; but, rather, to make the work itself the result of the treatment to which these objects are subjected. And, of course, these works have no relation to "scrap iron art," Pop art and other more-or-less faddish movements, although Felguérez could insert himself into these movements, giving them another meaning. In the mural at the Diana Cinema, for example, Felguérez has doubtlessly used forms in the rough, forms, we might say, that were suggested to him by the various fragments of scrap metal. But what matters is how Felguérez, basing himself on the fragments' inherent power of suggestion, organized and interconnected them according to a previously established, formal plan. In this way, the materials' power of suggestion is transformed into something else and put at the service of that scrupulously discovered plan, which is what gives the mural its true meaning. The result is the perfect unification through powerful rhythmic continuity of the mural's enormous space (30 x 5 meters), so that we confront a single composition standing unified within its diversity. And it is not strange that this composition displays characteristics very similar to those found with still greater frequency in the artist's earlier sculptures and paintings. Reappearing along the mural's expanse

is the same tendency to create groups of enveloping, self-containing forms, communicating with each other by means of a subtle balance, locking themselves in only to open up to another form until the entire work is integrated.

Through this process, Felguérez again demonstrates his old obsession with approaching the material and enclosing it within a strict boundary full of hidden implications so that the material itself will reveal to us its own power of expression within a harmonious order. At the same time, Felguérez's different murals also reveal a continual process of transformation, never in obedience to a system but always issuing in new creation. In this process, the varying nature of each material also plays its part. The tone of the works has changed, in a certain sense, in accordance with these materials. Thus, one of the two faces of the mural created for the Seattle Industrial Fair returns us to that integration of multiple, small planes characteristic of the painter's earlier canvases and has, moreover, the same brilliance of shades and tones. On the other hand, the mural for the private home on Felix Parra Street in Mexico City is based on the same construction material as the house itself and has the same ascetism, the same seriousness in the treatment of large planes and even the same treatment of the painstaking, extremely rich textures as paintings from Felguérez's black and white period. Also constructed with the same pleasure in the material's sensuous quality—sometimes reminiscent of Georges Braque—the mural is a perfect composition through whose serious tones and muffled harmonies the spiritual power of form shines with greater intensity than ever. Yet, in the mural at the Bahía swimming pool, form almost dissolves, changing into a delicate rhythmic continuity whose undulations extend for one hundred meters with neither visible point of departure nor final goal as they are transformed into an indivisible whole. And in the mural at the offices of the Confederation of Industrial Boards, that delicacy functions in the selection of forms. Polychromatic, the mural has a notable lightness in contrast to those at the Diana

Cinema or the house on Felix Parra, and Felguérez's use of plastic threads contributes to the assertion of that feeling. In the mural, Felguérez has tried to lighten the natural weightiness of iron and brass instead of affirming it. The objects' varying forms assume a fluttering gracefulness by means of which the spirit seems to rob the material of its attributes while the work as a whole —composed without break, almost completely avoiding the creation of separate planes—suggests precisely that desire to allow spirit, for once, to impose itself on matter rather than obliging spirit to be contained in matter, revealing that matter to us.

A new iron and glass mural in the Pedregal de San Juan district of Mexico City shows Felguérez's characteristic enveloping forms reappearing once again. The composition is at rest in a precise play of circles and semi-circles permitting the natural heaviness of the material to operate; but, in addition, the inclusion of glass tends to create a new element –light—that acts upon the iron through the glass. This combination un doubtedly suggests one of the constants running through the artist's work: heaviness of material and seriousness of forms on the one hand and fluttering gracefulness, the temptation of pure spirit, of yielding to the great enemy of material, on the other. Searching for the continual expression of that struggle, attempting to enclose matter in form and either compelling spirit to reveal itself to us or giving way to the impulse of arriving at spirit in its purest state, liberating energy merely by means of instinctive brush strokes and robbing volumes of their heaviness, Manuel Felguérez has already created a work whose authenticity and artistic merit are above reproach.

It is not odd that the presence of light in his most recent mural unequivocally influenced Felguérez when he returned to painting during a stay of several months in the United States. In the works he created there and continued under the same inspiration in Mexico, color seems to disclose its own transparency for the first time. These works are clearer and lighter than ever, not only in an external sense, but also, and above all, inwardly. Guided by this new element

in his palette—making it a painter's palette more surely than ever—Felguérez allows his traditional forms to be contaminated by a new lightheartedness. Consequently, a fresh enjoyment appears in the works, one that ultimately opens up the material, permitting within its closed boundary the celebration of transparency to create a new space where echoes of distant gardens and a remote evocation of nature filter through without modifying the abstract character of the forms, but conferring a new quality on them.

This evocation of nature in Felguérez's most recent painting is quickly converted into a candid celebration introducing a new and perturbing element into his work: eroticism. If up until now, as much in his painting as in his sculpture, the closed material always had a dark sensuality, a dense and ponderous weight born from taking pleasure in the material itself, that same sensuality now causes the material to encarnalize and reveal itself in a series of human figures that nevertheless are also no more than material—candid and impudent bodies exhibiting themselves only to themselves and concealing all their possible spirituality. On the other hand, spirituality becomes newly evident in the color, in the capacity of color to illuminate that inert flesh whose texture is closer to death than to life, as if the painter needed to abstract it from itself before bringing it to the work; but flesh, which in contrast to the transparency of the colors, takes on a spirituality not belonging to it but to the work.

Before this sudden appearance of a new element, apparently obliging the artist to fuse two aspects of his work in a distinct manner, it is only logical that the artist should have searched for a new formal solution to it. So, in his most recent works, Felguérez has finally joined that gravity of matter to the luminosity of spirit in a series of canvases that are as much sculpture—the volume of relief—as they are painting—reliefs united to the composition by means of color. Announced from the very beginning of his work, it is a natural result, but one that Felguérez has known how to await with exemplary patience. For greater unity, and paralleling his discovery of this au-

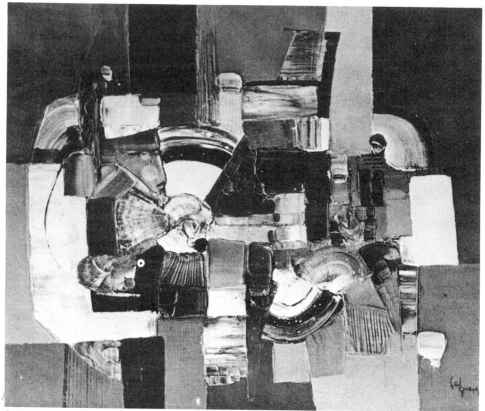

Composition I. 1959. Oil on canvas. 50 x 60 cm.

"Ciudad vertical." 1965. Oil on canvas. 95 x 80 cm.

"Antes del viaje." 1970. Mixed media. 100 x 80 cm.

"El paraíso de Hadaly." 1968. Oil on canvas. 60 x 150 cm.

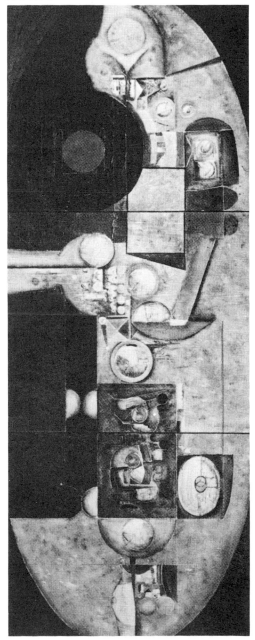

thentic sculpture-painting, the artist has learned to nullify the natural character that the appearance of human forms gives to the reliefs. He does this by abstracting the shapes from their own context and completely converting them into pure forms, by giving them the role of impersonal modules reappearing in the same form from one work to another. Felguérez accomplishes this in such a way that what establishes the particularity of each work within its unique composition is color as well as the play of light and shadow thus created and giving the material a distinct power in each painting. In this way, the work recognizes its single origin and at the same time unlocks variety without losing its own unique character. Examining the general development of Felguérez's work, it is easy to recognize this new solution as no merely formal variation, but as the creator's profound relationship to the elements nourishing his art. Thus, Felguérez has achieved the opening up of matter to its own immobile, indeterminate nature and, at the same time, given it a life that comes from outside. In his work, Felguérez has finally come to the absolute synthesis of that long dialogue between the closed, mute nature of matter and the struggle of spirit to reveal itself through matter. The truth of form conclusively opens form itself to the free access of truth, unsealing it for contemplation.

Is there any conclusion? The alternation through which the work of Manuel Felguérez has become visible has been nourished, from the outset, by the dialogue between matter and spirit that eventually opened into a continuity within which the very notion of dialogue is affirmed. Once the unity of each work as a closed creation—in whose interior space the creator's subjectivity lodges by being objectified—has been dismantled by the artist himself, the work apparently does not seek more than a proximity, a nearness, to its likeness in which it is reflected. Multiplication without center. There is no choice other than variation. Felguérez has finally chosen, if we pay attention to his latest exhibition at the Museo de Arte Moderno, repetition that is always difference. But it is necessary to

pause for a moment.

The movement within which the works of Manuel Felguérez are constituted has been uninterrupted in the direction of constructing, of realizing, as much in sculpture as in painting as in mural relief. Attraction to color, to textures, to volumes, and even to objects as objects. Always a space, but the artist was in the center, harmonizing the voices, determining the accent. The determination of form above the silence of the world, the spirit's murmuring in order to convert that silence into a voice keeping the truth of silence while revealing it; above the rhythm of the voice, an always inaudible murmuring, the silence of the world, which, when admitted, allows him or obliges him to resound over his material and, silencing it, preserve the voice's truth. We can also call the determination of form, of spirit, *idea*. Manuel Felguérez has maintained and nurtured an obsession with the value and place of idea within art, as if he feared its disappearance in the dense reality of the work, as if the work might destroy it, forcibly absorbing the idea that made it possible. And in the plastic arts the circumstance is that the idea does disappear, is converted into material, is materialized: such is creation's demand. What must be attacked, then, is the notion of the work as a unity within which everything is forfeited so the work may exist in its solitude. If we are allowed by appearance, which is what every work is, to turn from the work's closed presence toward its commentary in order to determine what elements constitute it and to trace the origins of the dialogue conducted within the artist and externalized in the work, then it is necessary to clear access to that dialogue as an indispensable part of art. And then the work also converts into a criticism of itself; it contains its own commentary on itself. Criticism of the creation in relation to a closed form, viewed as idea; but, equally, criticism of the idea as a pure, formless concept viewed as form, which that idea requires in order to reveal itself. Finally, creation and criticism joined in their separation, fixed in their diversity. An endless dialogue seeking no more.

In this sense, *Multiple Space*, as Manuel

Felguérez has correctly chosen to call his latest exhibition, is a dazzling construction of signs pointing nowhere else than to themselves. Reflection of reflections: opening its interiority, the work has shut itself again. But at that moment the value of repetition comes into play. As Felguérez himself says in the precise statement of his purposes: Felguérez seeks, "departing from a few simple geometric concepts . . . to produce a form-idea" that is basic. That form-idea is an arbitrarily chosen module, with no meaning or use beyond the combinational possibilities that the artist imagines in the forms he has chosen to constitute it. From that module the work begins to unfold as a multiplicity of variations, which, by reflecting each other repeat the central model but which also, finally, by means of their own appearance, nullify or destroy it: first a painting that multiplies itself in a seriograph showing it equal to itself within a different medium and therefore opening up an investigation into the unique character of its identity. In addition, the painting and the seriograph or the original module—it is all the same: the point of departure in each instance is further dissolved or reveals its irrelevance with greater clearness—later yield to what produces a relief from which, in turn, a sculpture is yet to be born. No longer has just the medium been modified, but also the volume in which the work manifests itself and which the work manifests. We find ourselves, precisely, confronting "multiple space." What is the center of that space? The answer can only be found at the heart of repetition and that repetition shows us—equalizing each work in its differences and destroying the closed nature of its supposedly unique character—that there is no center; there is a multiplicity through which the space becomes visible by means of the movement configuring it. Then the sign each work creates in the process of the work's being repeated and multiplied is forced by the artist to show that not only does each work not point toward any direction more than to itself, but also that it has no meaning beyond what it is given in its own appearance within space, which it affirms and which affirms it as a sign. That is,

the work lacks interiority; it is formed only by the exteriority revealing it and within that exteriority there is nothing. But as it unfolds in the space it makes possible, when it is repeated and multiplied, the sign also makes possible the movement of the space: the succession forming reality: a pure surface without depth, like the work of Manuel Felguérez. That dazzling and inexhaustible surface—on which all the colors, all the forms in their dimensions appear, doubling, repeating, multiplying, creating the radiance whereby the very splendor of the appearances making up the world manifests itself —that surface is, nevertheless, reality.

Every artist puts into his work the truth he has selected by means of the procedure he used to make that work possible. *Multiple Space* attacks and dissolves the notion of unique, closed work in order to replace it with a pure system of relations supporting each other and reflecting each other without any center; but in accomplishing that, it also attacks and dissolves the notion of the work's author. The artist does not discover a meaning, which he then makes evident by converting the work into its representation. Rather, he starts out from the absence of all meaning, indicates the work itself when it nullifies itself as a unique sign and discovers its truth in the repetition reflecting it and which it reflects. The artist is going to discover his own identity in the work. Instead of giving that identity to the work, he waits for the work to deliver it to him. And the work surrenders its absence of meaning to him: the negation of all identity. A journey from one nothing to another nothing. The author can only be found in his disappearance within the series. We find ourselves looking at the thought of no one, which someone has succeeded in making present by means of the form-idea, assenting to thought's thinking him. Thus, the exhibition definitively dislodges the painter from himself.

Only in these terms can we find the meaning in the beauty of the forms that *Multiple Space* proposes to us. That beauty rests in neutrality. No subjectivity nourishes it. Each color, each form, each volume could be another; their value is a value of relation.

There is no original point of departure since there is no origin. Instead there is a causality determining the creation of the module where the form-idea reveals itself precisely out of the neutrality of "a few simple geometric concepts." And, in fact, each color, each form, each volume is many others, as the exhibition demonstrates to us in the neighboring series based on the same principle. The whole creates the mirroring surface that is *Multiple Space*. Within that surface each painting, each seriograph, each relief, each sculpture is a radiance surging and standing forth like foam building up the crest of waves in the sea; but each work has no value, no meaning other than this particular intensity, which is only possible within the totality of a movement without beginning or end. Suddenly departing from a point that is impossible to situate, the dialogue between matter and spirit, between form and idea, returns, recommences, repeats itself as a continual murmuring in whose density lodges the acute sublimity that is each work. To provoke that sublimity, which forfeits him and in which he forfeits himself, is the exalted task of the artist Manuel Felguérez.

This essay as well as the Chronology were originally published in García Ponce's book, *Felguérez*, as part of the UNAM's series on artists (Mexico City, 1976).

"Disminución del tiempo." 1975. Enamel on canvas. 100 x 120 cm.

Of Space and Time:

An Interview with Manuel Felguérez and Mayer Sasson

ROBERT A. PARKER

The Mexican artist Manuel Felguérez has for nearly three decades explored the language of space in his work. From the early sculptures of the 1950s, to huge murals in relief in the 1960s, to his current efforts at merging the two-dimensional and three-dimensional worlds into what he terms "multiple space," he has been manipulating reality in search of a new esthetic vision.

Expressed in its simplest terms, the content of Felguérez's work consists of geometric shapes. His work, he acknowledges, has been strongly influenced by the visual images of today's technology. Within the past year, indeed, he has taken a major step in his efforts to express the unique elements comprising reality—form, color, texture, proportion, and dimension—by combining them in two dimensions so that, in the words of Octavio Paz, multiple spaces "unfold silently in front of us and are transformed into another space . . . [until] spaces literally create and construct themselves before our eyes."

Since he works with symbols of the scientific world—the circle, the triangle, the square—it should be no surprise that Felguérez believes science to be a basic ingredient of our culture. But his decision to use its technology may have been truly inevitable. Thus, almost as if he has measured the number of creative years that re-

main to him, Felguérez has at age 48 turned to the computer. He may in fact be the first artist to employ a space-age machine in order to collapse the time necessary for his explorations.

Felguérez's work has been exhibited in Europe, Latin America, and the United States for twenty years. In 1975, he won the Grand Award of Honor at the XIII Diennial Exhibition of São Paulo, Brazil. Last year, he received a Guggenheim Fellowship to attend the Carpenter Center for Visual Arts at Harvard University and continue his computerized explorations of "multiple space." He met with limited success, however, until a visit to New York City, where he encountered an old acquaintance, Mayer Sasson. An electrical engineer by profession, Sasson, a Colombian, has an international reputation. He has published nearly fifty papers on a variety of computer-related topics and has participated in international conferences and seminars in London, Barcelona, Bucharest, São Paulo, and New York. Early in 1976 their collaboration began, and in December the first results were placed on exhibit at the Carpenter Center in Cambridge, Massachusetts.

While Felguérez's use of the computer should not be permitted to overshadow the esthetic achievement of his work, its use does satisfy the artist's own criterion than an object of art include the characteristic of *novedad* or newness: Felguérez's technique may well turn out to be revolutionary in the history of art.

ROBERT A. PARKER is Manager of Communications for the public accounting firm of Touche Ross & Co. and editor of its two magazines.

Why did you turn to the computer in your work?

Felguérez: There are two reasons. First, by 1967 my approach to art was based on the construction of certain geometric shapes. Now, when you work with geometry you begin with mathematics, and what better instrument is there than the computer for dealing with the world of mathematics? Second, I was then lecturing at the University of Mexico. In teaching art, there are two sides, what we might term the rational and the irrational. The irrational you cannot teach; that is sensitivity. But you can teach the rational side of art, and doing so impressed me with the fact that I was using logic and mathematics. So, thinking of my style in mathematical terms, I began to wonder if somehow the computer could help me. I was not sure what it would actually do; it was more a choice made by intuition. However, before I actually used a computer, there were three years of slow analysis. And before I began to work with Mayer another three years went by.

What do you say to people who consider the computer a crutch, an illegitimate tool for an artist?

Felguérez: That's a common reaction. And if it were the machine creating the work, yes, it would be illegitimate. But if the computer can serve *my* creativity, what is wrong with that? When an engineer or scientist uses a computer to increase his creativity, no one objects. It is recognized that the machine is creative because the man using it is creative. Now, if it can have its own artificial intelligence when run by a person of intelligence, then might not the artist, a man of sensibility, seek a way to put that sensitivity into the computer? I believe so. And I believe the success of our work, the originality of our work, the realization of our work has followed the feeding of something completely subjective into the computer.

There's no possibility the computer can influence your ideas more than you intend?

Felguérez: No, because from the start in Mexico, I intended to make contact with the computer through my style. Now, an artist's style is as characteristic as his fingerprints. You can say in music, well, this is Mozart, or this is Bach. And in art you cannot mistake an El Greco or a Goya. So I began by trying to find the characteristics that define my style. Good or bad style, it didn't matter; what mattered was that after twenty-five years of creating art, my work had a language, a syntax that I alone used. And it seemed to me that if I could put the combination of elements comprising my style into the computer, that if I confined it strictly to those limits, then the computer could not invent anything new. It was blocked from going beyond that point.

Sasson: Two comments. It is blocked, yes, Manuel, but there would still be a way for the computer to break out of the limits of your style. That is, just as your ideas may change from year to year as a result of a prior experience you had not considered before, so the computer may discover possibilities that are actually yours, because you fed the information into it, but that had never come together in your mind. The second point is that most people consider the computer only as an apparatus that can perform very fast mathematical calculations. But what the public does not know is that the computer can follow any logical process of ideas. For example, one can use it to study philosophy, because philosophy is based on logic, and logic is nothing else but mathematics, and mathematics is the world of the computer. So with the computer, one can do the most basic type of thinking. Conceptually, there is no difference between saying that three is larger than two and saying that A is different from B, or idea A is more general than idea B. For the ideas relate to one another in the same way that numbers do. I wish I could be clearer, because it has always been a problem for me to explain this to people who are highly intelligent in other fields but who close their minds completely when I try to tell them that important aspects of

A common language had to be established in order to communicate with the computer. Felguérez realized that with the eight basic elements shown above he could describe more than twenty years of his artistic production.

how a man thinks can be expressed in the world of mathematics.

So how did you both go about reducing Felguérez's art to mathematical elements?

Sasson: The solution was not to analyze Manuel's style in order to discover its essential features, which is what he had been doing, since that meant defining a myriad of intangible laws. We took the opposite approach of observing his prior works and building a model from a synthesis of its many parts. This is called *system identification.*

Felguérez: I had discovered in Mexico that all my geometric constructions could be reduced to fifteen basic shapes. And after years of analysis, I had learned that the greatest number of circles I had used in one work was, let's say, ten, and the fewest number was two; that the maximum number of rectangles I'd put in one work was fifteen and the minimum five. And I had also studied the relative size of each shape, the largest and smallest I'd used, and the position of each in the frame. What was fascinating about this was that an artist works intuitively and so I'd never known such data about my work. Until I talked to Mayer, however, I had found it difficult to translate all this into a mathematical language. It was his idea, for example, that in working with a square in two-dimensional space and a cube in three-dimensional space, we could determine the coordinates of where the shape is by means of two numbers for a square and three numbers for a cube. And we could program the size by numbers for the height and width, or height, width, and depth. Today, as Mayer suggested earlier, this identification of the

Applying the common language to nine of his prior works, we produced the drawings shown above. These, and others like them, were communicated to the computer to be studied with the system identification method in order to arrive at mathematical equations (model) that represented the esthetic substance of Felguérez's style.

system that exists in my mind has led to a new richness in my work that I hadn't known existed within me.

Sasson: The computer is like a new pair of eyes for seeing inside you.

When and why did you begin to discuss all this with Mayer?

Felguérez: In 1975, I had created my first work with the computer in Mexico, but there were certain defects I could not resolve. So I obtained a Guggenheim Fellowship to go to Cambridge, where MIT and Harvard are located and where I could use the maximum computer technology in the United States. When I was visiting New York and saw Mayer was interested in what I was doing, I set some "traps" to get him involved. Actually, it was ideal, for we spoke the same language in more ways than one.

Mayer, what did you think of Felguérez's idea?

Sasson: Well, I could immediately translate his uncertainties into my own uncertainties in computer research. He was searching for what I myself am normally seeking in my work, and it was doubly stimulating because, frankly, a specialist in my type of work has very few people he can talk to intensely about what he's doing. And of course, I had been interested in art for many years, because that's my wife's profession. On one visit, Manuel spent the night with us after an evening of talk, and I awoke early the next morning and did some calculations. Then, very timidly at breakfast, fearful I might offend him because I might seem to be trying to take something away from him, I asked if he would mind some suggestions and he said he'd mind only if I did *not* show him my ideas.

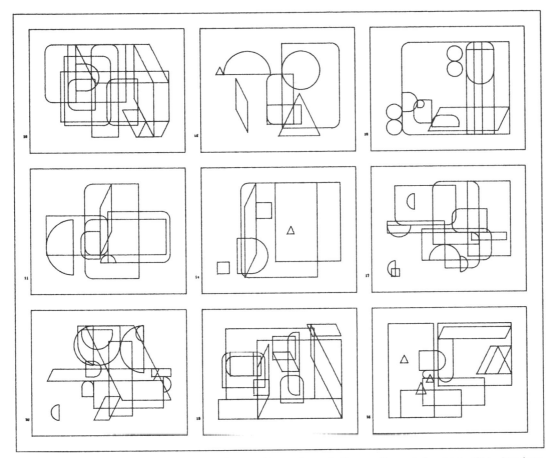

The identified model can only communicate with us through the medium of drawings. The drawings above were produced in the computer by the model based upon everything the computer had learned about the esthetics of Felguérez.

Felguérez: We worked on the initial concept mostly by mail, Mayer in New York and I at Harvard. As I said, I had already analyzed 300 of my paintings to find the fifty with the greatest differences, so that the model we created would reflect the widest panorama of my capacity to invent geometric shapes. We then reduced my fifteen basic shapes to just eight, and for each of the fifty works I had to reduce the number, size, and position of each of the new basic shapes to numerals, using the system Mayer had devised. I would send him the numbers, and then Mayer's computer program would convert the numbers into fifty sketches, which I would review for accuracy. After about three months, we had the twenty-five years of my work summed up in the computer as a group of equations—called a mathematical model—and we then instructed the computer, working within my style, to create the first group of new drawings in accord with the rules of the model.

I might compare this next stage to a comet approaching the earth. The astronomical observatory, by taking down all its data for the next eight days—the only time the comet will be visible—predicts the comet's path for thousands of years. And so the fifty sketches were like observing eight days of my work.

Sasson: Once we had the mathematical model of the fifty prior works, we asked the computer to produce the first *idea-forms* —or line drawings—which we arbitrarily limited to 208. It was a very emotional moment for me when we obtained the first results, because until that moment it was all theory. But when Manuel looked at the first computer drawings and said, "This is my world," I knew we had achieved success. Then it became a matter of Manuel selecting fifty-four of the 208 drawings and working on each one to define it artistically. Then we fed these fifty-four new works,

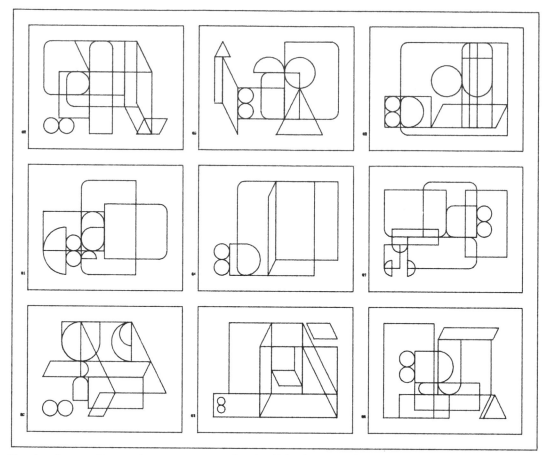

The drawings on the previous page were taken by Felguérez to be idea-forms or sketches that required his further work. The corresponding drawings on this page show what finally resulted after Felguérez reacted to the models' indications.

which represented new information for the computer, back into the machine along with the fifty prior works. From this feedback, the computer produced 208 new drawings, each representing an enrichment that Manuel found closer to his actual style, and from this new group Manuel chose to work on seventy-two that he sensed had the greatest esthetic possibilities.

How does your mind work, Manuel, when you begin to transform the computer drawings into creative works?

Felguérez: One way is emotional and the other is rational. From the set of 208 drawings the computer gives me, I decide which ones are most pleasing to me, and this decision is strictly emotional, strictly subjective. Because I really do not know why I like this one and not that one. But once I make the choice, the rational part begins.

That is, this circle that is here, I would like to have there. And while I like the size of that square subjectively, at the same time rationally, for composition, it has to be smaller. Finally, I decide which drawings are worth spending the weeks or a month I'll need to create each painting or sculpture.

How are you going to find the time, if you are, to work on all the drawings you select? Of the first 122 idea forms, you only exhibited eighteen oils and ten metal sculptures at Harvard.

Felguérez: It would be a marketing problem if I could work as fast as the computer. It produces a line drawing in ten seconds. But what will probably happen is that I will become bored after a few more paintings, and I will certainly be changing my ideas anyway. So there will be new information to feed into the computer, and I will in turn receive back new *idea-forms,* or drawings, that will stimulate me again. Thus, we create a system, break the system, create a system, break the system, and by this constant change the system remains alive and my creativity is continually challenged.

What new directions do you see for your work with the computer?

Sasson: The drawings are schematic now, meaning you see only the outline of the shapes. But we could introduce more drawing elements, for example shadings or texture, so there would be a richer surface, perhaps adding sculptural elements, another dimension.

Felguérez: Before I started using the computer, I was beginning to work out how the two-dimensional shapes I was using in my style could become three-dimensional through the logic of their construction. That's why I exhibited at Harvard not only paintings but sculptures—in order to demonstrate how the *idea-forms,* the drawings, could develop in space. So, I will probe more deeply into my theory of multiple space. But it's not only in art that these developments might take place. There are also people even now who are investigating the possibilities of the computer in music, and even in poetry. And they are getting closer and closer to their objective. But I believe ours is the first case in which anyone has demonstrated the actual esthetic capacity of the computer.

Sasson: Yet it is quite possible that as we talk another artist with another computer engineer is attacking the same problem in a different way that will open up even more areas than Manuel and I have done.

What is the future of your approach to art? If times change, will it lose its validity?

Felguérez: That's a question no one can answer. At least it will be an example of what was done in the 20th century. But I do know that on showing my "computer" work to the critics, those who knew my work saw everything as a logical development. They did not say, how new, how different, for the computer process did not matter to them. There was the surprise, yes, that is in every new work of art, but they recognized that the work was mine. It still used balance and simplicity of shapes, as they relate to one another in size and color, to create a harmony, like a musical harmony, that has no symbolic meaning, that is simply esthetically pleasing to the eye.

So you're saying it is your art itself that's going to determine its validity in the future.

Felguérez: Yes, I have never wanted to believe that a work of art should need an explanation, such as the process that was used to create it. On the other hand, when you are viewing a Greek vase created 800 years before Christ, I do accept that understanding the historical and cultural context of its origin can enrich the appreciation you already have.

Sasson: In our case, however, it is disconcerting to many that a computer brings the enrichment. It is something different, and people today don't want to stop and try to understand what an artist is trying to achieve. They forget that each work comes out of an artist's entire experience, that the creative process is usually the result of many complex factors maturing slowly in the artist's mind. They want to look and to understand a thing at once.

Felguérez: History has taught us that the one who understands is the one who is interested beforehand. That is, the first people to discover a new composer are the composers, and the first to discover an artist are the artists. Why? Because they understand not only the result but the process as well.

Sasson: And what follows is usually a period of time in which the work of art reaches its true value on its own.

Felguérez: Currently, however, our work is too new to have reached such a stage. ⭕

Series "La Máquina Estética"

1. Computer drawing

2. Oil on canvas

3. Metal sculpture

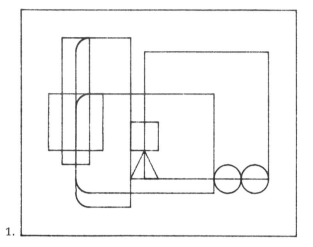

1.

2.

3.

Buñuel in Mexico

E. RUBINSTEIN

Saint Cinema

Because we're all auteurists now—so Andrew Sarris counsels and cautions us, and who but Gore Vidal would still find it amusing to call the point in question?—we flock in astonishing numbers to such events as MOMA's 1976 retrospective of the films Luis Buñuel made in Mexico between 1947 and 1961, the year the great commercial success of *Viridiana* re-established him as an "international" director. The auditorium is nearly filled at two o'clock of a bitter Tuesday afternoon in January for the second of two showings of a beggarly little melodrama called *El bruto* (1953), screened in a print innocent of even an occasional English subtitle to make us feel wanted. And we find what we have come for, tiny pieces of the jigsaw of the maestro's career. Katy Jurado turns up in unusually ugly shoes: what quaint allusion to his signature fetish is Buñuel insinuating? The same lady plunges

E. RUBINSTEIN, the author of critical studies on Jane Austen and Buster Keaton, teaches film in the Divison of Humanities of Richmond College.

her finger into a glass of tequila, then straight into the eager mouth of a wondrously desiccated old man; and later, our good Senior Citizen all but trips over his son's mutilated corpse on his way to steal a sweet from a cabinet. Deep in the pits of the Mexican movie industry, an industry unredeemed even by Hollywood's technical riches, a great *cinéaste* causes his wickedest self to be projected.

Shot in less than three weeks, and, according to Buñuel, shot in disregard of some of his own dearest wishes, *El bruto* can fitly represent the species of film that gives the retrospective its *raison d'être*. The manifestly "personal" Buñuelian testimonies that issued from his Mexican years—*Los olvidados* (1950), *El* (1953), *Ensayo de un crimen* (1955), *Nazarín* (1959)—are by now pretty standard North American art-house fare (and because of this, I'll have little to say of them); the singularity of the MOMA enterprise lies in the exhumation of Buñuel's generally unknown Mexican studio assignments. These are, in large part, comedies and melodramas in the official Mexican national manner, many of which were understandably denied wide commercial release in non-Spanish-speaking countries. Still, none of these will entirely disappoint you, not if you watch with expectations of rewards no grander than the reward of rediscovering Buñuel amidst all the banalities, all the longueurs, all the crudities of production. (And isn't this the very reward which, by Sarris' principle, defines The Way We Live Now?) In one of several memorable sequences of *La ilusión viaja en tranvía* (1954), for example, you will see various parts of various slaughtered beasts dangling not in an abattoir but from the baggage racks in a streetcar; in *El río y la muerte* (1955), you will see a man in an iron lung having his face slapped. No need to try to explain the way in which the plots of these films are made to house such fierce, liberating visions; let the visions stand sufficient unto their maker.

And for all the unique power of these and countless other images, more powerful still in its uniqueness is the inescapable myth of this maker.

San Luis

The arts of our century have engendered few figures as heroic as Luis Buñuel. What our experience has given us to hate, Buñuel has hated publicly and fiercely, from the addictive goo served up by all the movie industries to the despotisms of Spain and Latin America to the God who let this century happen, finally to you and me because, if only for a moment, we may have permitted ourselves, or may someday permit ourselves, to be tempted by candy any child can see is poisoned. Behind the timely scandals of his work with Dali, behind the listless heavings and posturing on view in his worst Mexican movies, behind the sexy French color photography of *Belle de Jour* and *Le Charme discret*—behind whatever seems dated or trivial or too inviting in his films—looms the figure of the existential hero of the cinema.

To enlist this intransigent, irrefragable giant in your party is plainly to certify the justness of your claims on truth; and if your inclinations lead you leftward, you'll soon discover that somewhere along the path of his career the giant has spoken out in a voice you can appropriate. There exists scarcely an extremist position, scarcely a "style of radical will" that can be called utterly foreign to Buñuel. His contempt for the pretensions of sanity demands that he expose all the deceptions and rationalizations of the international cabal of the bourgeoisie, his scorn of the bourgeoisie demands that he demonstrate its indispensability to the prosperity of international fascism, his horror of fascism demands that he anatomize the self-protective strategies of the Church, his anti-clericalism locates him in the Goyesque tradition of Spanish painting, his place in that tradition necessitates his commitment to the spirit of uncompromised art, that commitment calls for the spreading of the word of Surrealism—and Surrealist principles lead to the savaging of the pretensions of sanity. My formulation doesn't aim at completeness.

Further, the very trimness of my formulation is deceptive. Buñuel's career stands not for an achieved annularity but for an ideal, inaccessible integrity. Buñuel, moreover, is always set to overthrow by violence whatever system of ideas appears just now to be supporting him: we have, if we need it, Buñuel's own word that deeper than his allegiance to Breton or to Freud or to Marx is his allegiance to rebellion. Beware, then, of those doctrinaire critics of whatever calling who will have you believe that even in Mexico Buñuel hardly paused in the making of masterpieces. Like the slum-sapped faces in *Los olvidados,* the Mexican films speak frequently of the deprivations of their provenance. Ideological cosmetics won't hide the marks of malnutrition.

Nor are the insufficiencies of most of the Mexican productions to be understood only with respect to the limitations of the Mexican industry. Buñuel directed these productions as he directs everything: with a meanness I'm not tempted to qualify as scrupulous. An Ophüls, to seek an illustration at the far end of the gamut, could bring to an incongruous Hollywood script a visual wisdom that rains grace on every frame: Buñuel, with that unaccommodating journeyman competence that is, in two senses of the phrase, his pride, encourages an incongruous script to enact its own weaknesses and follies for all to see. Ophüls, by virtue of fixing so plainly the distance between the ostensible subject and the subject transfigured, generates a relatively easy, hospitable irony that allows for our knowing participation in the controlling spirit of his work; Buñuel autographs a film most unmistakably by means of sudden epiphanic lightning bolts that fade the dreary stuff around them in ratio to their own savage brilliance.

And Buñuel's attitude toward actors borders on the savage as well, as Pauline Kael (in *Going Steady*) knows:

From the casting and the listless acting in many of his movies, one can conclude only that he's unconcerned about such matters; often he doesn't seem to bother even to cast for type, and one can't easily tell if the characters are meant to be what they appear to be. He uses actors in such an indifferent way that they scarcely even stand for the characters. Rather than allow the bad Mexican actors that he generally works with to act, he seems to dispense with acting by just rushing them through their roles without giving them time to understand what they're doing. Clearly, he prefers no acting to bad acting.

I'd modify Kael's judgments in two regards: not all his Mexican actors are bad, while not all his bad actors are Mexican; and if indeed Buñuel prefers no acting to bad acting, his preference isn't always honored.

Though *The Young One* (1960) is in many ways atypical of Buñuel's Mexican work (it was shot in English; it was released in North America; it even turns up on U.S. television), it may, because of its relative familiarity, furnish a helpful illustration. The principal figures are the gamekeeper of a Southern coastal island (Zachary Scott), a recently-orphaned adolescent girl who is the island's only other permanent tenant (Kay Meersman), and a Northern black jazz musician (Bernie Hamilton) who, accused of raping a white woman during a visit to a mainland town, flees in a small boat and seeks out the island for temporary shelter; these three are later joined by a preacher (Claudio Brook) whose job it is to baptize the girl and a ferryman (Crahan Denton) whose joy it is to torture the black in anticipation of the festive lynching to come. The point of departure is the conflict among four versions of negritude, that of the cracker gamekeeper who has always assumed the uniform inferiority of "niggers," that of a racially color-blind child, that of a preacher whose infinite regard for Negro souls is tempered by his refusal to sleep on the black man's bed until the mattress has been turned, and that of a redneck confirmed in sadism. But the situation is complicated by the gamekeeper's lust for the girl. Twice he seduces her; his crimes discovered by the preacher, he begins to sense the meaning of moral and social exclusion, and so attains new understanding of the black man's condition.

Buñuel scores more than enough points to contest the simplistic liberal schematization with which the script threatens us: I'm thinking of the contrast between the girl's unwelcome baptismal immersion at the hands of the preacher and the girl's rather less unwelcome introduction into deeper waters at the hands of the gamekeeper; of the outfit—including, Buñuel being Buñuel, oversize high-heeled shoes—that the gamekeeper brings the girl from town both to sap her resistance and to render her a publicly fit object of lust; and of the erotic spell the black man casts on the island with his clarinet solo as he pauses from protesting that he never raped anyone. And there are, as always, fleeting unforgettable images, best of all the image of a bottle of whiskey solemnly planted by the girl in the earth over her father's grave. Much less happy is the basic proposition of the swiftness of the gamekeeper's moral awakening, a phenomenon painfully akin to the kind of ninety-minute Hollywood psychiatric cure that Buñuel himself mocks so knowingly in *Ensayo de un crimen*. But even this weakness isn't fatal. It's the "direction" of the actors, pitiful creatures cast adrift in Buñuel's frames, that subverts the effect of the movie.

Scott, never an actor to be tainted by subtlety, is here merely left to his own devices and so rehearses every tic, every hyperthyroid glance at his disposal. Hamilton realizes neither the superficially defiant black buckishness nor the profound black anguish his wretchedly-written role seems to demand. Brook, later so memorable, in his hairy gauntness as Simon of the Desert, here quite understandably misses every nuance of the running-water-Baptist voice (but less understandably sounds always as though he'll find his verbal home not in Spanish but in some Teutonic tongue). And muttering little Kay Meersman, in the most difficult and ambiguous part in the film, possesses neither the skills of a professional actress nor the sheer disquieting presentness of a being like Bresson's Mouchette. Actors like these don't stand a chance with Buñuel, and the situation is no different with most of Buñuel's all-Mexican casts. Yes, I understand that I should—and think I do—appreciate the director's unwillingness to promote cozy sympathy for his characters, but I also believe that the annihilation of the actors is a dear price to pay for the degree of alienation Buñuel insists on.

Yet for all the shortness of interest in his own film that his response to his players might otherwise imply, Buñuel honors *The Young One* with some of the most impressive narrative editing of his career. Especially in the first third, which is given over to exposing and interlocking the situation of the island residents and the situation of the black fugitive, the director operates as if the squandering of even one frame, let alone one shot, would mean his death; here if anywhere is meaningful evidence of his esteem for Hollywood professionalism. The pieces fall together at once so tellingly and with such frugality that you realize that the sequence must have been conceived in every detail long before the shooting. Hence the pertinence of these words of Oscar Dancigers, the producer of most of Buñuel's Mexican films: after announcing that "directing is the easiest part of film work and anybody can do it," Dancigers adds that "I consider, and so does Buñuel, that the genuine director is at the same time a writer, an author. Buñuel is that kind. The essential part of the film is finished for him before the actual directing begins. That is only a simple matter of execution, and he is most impatient to get it finished and done with as soon as possible, which explains the astounding speed of his shooting." These views may be as shocking to today's director-crazed audience as any fantasy in any Buñuel film; but, provided only that we allow "authorship" to encompass mental editing as well as scripting, the evidence of the Mexican pictures allows one to believe that Dancigers speaks the truth about Buñuel's procedures. Buñuel's "impatience" on the set, his apparent refusal to concern himself with such details as the ability of the actors to speak to one another, is still plainer in his Mexican work than elsewhere.

But for all this, such is the force of Buñuel's presence that even as I market my skill in weighing his failures against his strengths, I worry that I have betrayed myself into an act of public foolishness. Don't Buñuel's failures—I'm speaking now of failures I take to be born of his own perversity, not born of the conditions under which he made films like *Gran casino* and *El bruto*

and *The Young One*, though in the end the distinction probably doesn't matter—don't Buñuel's failures finally confuse all my customary responses, whether of compassion or of condescension, to failure? If Buñuel forces me to question whether my responses aren't rooted in precisely the bourgeois esthetics he's teaching me to despise, how can I deny him the right to force me to assign greater meaning to the question than to the answer? Am I seriously asking that splendid taurine head of Buñuel's to bow to *my* notion of the attentions a film deserves?

In Buñuel's case, one's questions are one's homage; and with questions one can live more peacefully than with the claims promoted by those critics who act as though simply getting through some of Buñuel's Mexican films presented no difficulties; and those critics who read a film like *The Young One* as a Marxist allegory of quite uncanny subtlety; and those critics who seize upon Buñuel's atheism with sophomoric glee, imply atheism to be Buñuel's private discovery, and allow atheism to obscure, or even justify, Buñuel's every weakness. Buñuel's weaknesses are neither to be denied, nor masked, nor, even with respect to the Mexican films, always ascribed with a knowledgeable shrug to others. His weaknesses are his, manifestations of that sheer refusal to accommodate an audience that is his most salutary trait. Buñuel would not be himself if he gave us what we want, nor would we be the audience he wants if we failed to protest.

Some Versions of Purgatory

As sharply as the melodramas or farces on contemporary Mexican themes, Buñuel's adaptations of two classics of English fiction reveal the unanticipated rewards and unanticipated frustrations, the *splendeurs et misères*, of Buñuel's work of the fifties. One is *Abismos de pasión* (for by this title Latin American audiences were supposed to recognize *Wuthering Heights*), a great rarity and one of the MOMA show's welcome gifts. The other is the familiar *Robinson*

Crusoe (1952), renewed in value to the Museum public because seen at last in its most meaningful context.

Abismos de pasión exemplifies the cool, limited professional methods which Buñuel so admired in American movies and which Buñuel himself mastered in the years following *Los olvidados* when he turned out at least two products annually for the Mexican industry. Here as everywhere, Buñuel in placing his camera opts most often for what Sarris (in *Interviews with Film Directors*) calls "a middle distance, too close for cosmic groupings and too far away for self-identification." Set-ups are relatively few; when the camera pans, or, as occurs less frequently in this film, when the camera travels, it isn't in order to explore the cinematic field but, seemingly, in order to permit the actors some movement without necessitating a new take. Sharp cutting takes precedence over potentially evocative dissolves and potentially portentous fades (unless my memory fails, the screen never goes dark in a film called *Abismos de pasión!*). In sum, the story gets told with minimal challenge to Hollywood's version of cinematic normality. (Significantly, Buñuel's major departure from Hollywood business-as-usual lies in his customary choice of a deep focus within any given field. But as a rule the effect of this choice isn't what one would look for—that is, the effect of this choice isn't to equate the freedom of camera eye and human eye to reorganize photographed space, but rather to disavow the sovereignty of the dominant figures in the frame, to democratize the elements within the composition; in Hollywood, for obvious reasons, adjustments in focus were needed to assure the supremacy of figure over ground, of star over scene. Buñuel's major departure is thus in the direction of even weaker commitment to the romantic possibilities of his subjects.)

There's nothing wrong with these methods (in part because there's nothing intrinsically wrong with *any* methods), and they are exactly suited to at least one aspect—the most celebrated aspect—of Buñuel's work. Not for Buñuel, or at least rarely, the vertiginous prospects, the spatial disloca-tions, the visual oratory of Orson Welles. For Buñuel, nightmare is born out of the novel arrangement of visual data, not out of novelty of perspective. When Buñuel moves us into fantasy, daydream, hallucination, he seldom calls for adjustment of our sights. For all his talk of "poetic" cinema, Buñuel likes his horrors and wonders in prose, seen straight on and at eye level. And when, at the end of *Abismos de pasión*, Buñuel awakens to Emily Brontë, he asserts the validity of his style as forcefully as anywhere.

Heathcliff has pursued dead Catherine to the crypt that holds her coffin; Hindley, shotgun in hand, has pursued Heathcliff; Hindley's last gesture of vengeance will be to abort Heathcliff's last gesture of love. Already bleeding from the first blast of the gun, Heathcliff attempts to make love to Catherine's corpse. He looks up to the doorway of the crypt (it's a low-angle shot, but natural here, serving only to fix Heathcliff's point of vision): there he sees Catherine, in white, beckoning him—toward what? The figure of Catherine is replaced by the figure of Hindley. Another blast tears apart Heathcliff's face. He tumbles backwards onto Catherine's body.

Emily Brontë doesn't end her story this way (nor does she begin her story, as Buñuel does, with the return of Heathcliff from his voyage into the world), but she does make clear that a necrophiliac act, *because* a necrophiliac act, is Heathcliff's way to express the fanaticism of his love. Brontë would have seen that an image of Catherine in vestal attire but making seductive gestures is interchangeable on every level with an image of Hindley's gun. She would have recognized the symbolic aptness of the disfigurement that leads to Heathcliff's final convulsion. And the novelist who herself caused her wonderful tale to be narrated in a prose that keeps close to Victorian norms would have agreed that, to bring to an audience an episode like this one, a film director must do as little as he knows how to draw attention to himself. Buñuel's objectivity here is his testimony to the very actuality of those lunatic forces that drive his characters.

When, however, Buñuel's material is intrinsically less compelling, or when, as in most of *Abismos de pasión*, Buñuel's own commitment is faint—twenty years earlier Buñuel had wished to bring to the screen Brontë's adumbration of the Surrealist doctrine of *l'amour fou*, but when the occasion finally presented itself his interest had plainly withered—then Buñuel's style serves to bleed every shot of excitement. Whole sequences begin and proceed and then end without a visual accent or a shift in visual rhythm to recompense the eye. The black-and-white cinematography looks as dull as those of most of Buñuel's Mexican movies (though I admit that the 16mm print shown at the Museum makes this a point of conjecture). And, needless to say, the performances are intolerable, with Buñuel giving no sign of wishing to rescue a Heathcliff (a Heathcliff here renamed Alejandro: as well rename the house he lives in Clearview Manor) whose widely-noted resemblance to Farley Granger constitutes not his big drawback but his crucial talent, or a Catherine who is similarly drawn on Hollywood models of the day (School of Terry Moore) and who into the bargain speaks *very* funny

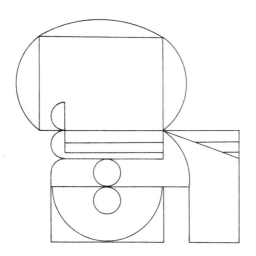

Spanish. It's true, as Buñuel's admirers never tire of pointing out, that almost nowhere in the Goldwynized *Wuthering Heights* does William Wyler come as close to the spirit of Brontë's moorish raptures and cruelties as Buñuel sporadically in the course of *Abismos de pasión* and then, overpoweringly, at the end; but Gregg Toland's photography and Olivier's Heathcliff and even Merle Oberon's Cathy of the Porcelain Brow are consistently about *something*. In Mexico, Buñuel found the technical means to achieve a plane of sheer tedium beyond the reach of most directors.

If Buñuel shows himself hesitant to honor Emily Brontë with a film that demonstrates at very least an uninterruptedly lively sympathy for her imagined world, what might one expect of his version of a novel by Daniel Defoe? Between Brontë and Buñuel there exist evident affinities. The novelist who envisions an arm being drawn again and again over jagged glass calls out clearly to the filmmaker who introduced himself to the world in *Un Chien andalou* with the image of a razor slitting an eyeball. Both Brontë and Buñuel hunger for emotional harvests that only the bleakest of natural landscapes will yield. Both Brontë and Buñuel lay bare romantic agitations that defy, or transcend, or simply ignore any of the more common genital appeasements. But what has Buñuel to share with Defoe? What could the master of hallucination discover in the pages of the master of catalogues? How but with a contempt at once too easy and too familiar could Buñuel show us the sullen faith and the bare capitalist face of old Crusoe?

Buñuel, as he must, ignores our questions and confounds our expectations. In one way, however, if in only one way, he does honor our assumptions about the nature of a Buñuelian reworking of Defoe: he is at his most eloquent where the destitute rhetoric of Defoe's bourgeois Puritanism falls short, namely with respect to what we take to be the emotional reality of Crusoe's awful isolation. Buñuel's Crusoe enters the surf, torch in hand, as though prepared to walk through oceans to find other people; Buñuel's Crusoe plants himself on his Echo Mountain to bellow the Twenty-third Psalm, filling the air with God's phrases, because those are the phrases that are supposed to help, filling the air too with human voices because those are what he needs to hear, even if they're only reverberations of his own. (But all voices cease when the terrible echoing words "my soul" have *become* Crusoe's island.) And Buñuel's Crusoe isn't bereft of fellowship alone. He reacts with heavy heart to the sight of a woman's gown he salvaged from the ship now draped on a scarecrow; he later reacts with genuine horror when Friday, who from his advent on the island has been seen in shoulder-length hair and long skirts, at last enters freely into female identity by dressing up for an intimate dinner with his master in another reclaimed female gown and a necklace of reclaimed gold coins, all the while lost in delirious laughter as he slashes the air with a great sword. (Shades—what shades—of Sabu: whoever invented The Elephant Boy decades earlier could hardly have had in mind this show of *all* the perverse implications of the little pet savage.)

These sequences are among the most striking in the film—are among its anthology pieces—but they're also part of a coherent whole in their final effect: they serve Buñuel's unlooked-for plan to make of Crusoe an available figure of sympathy. Buñuel, for example, pushes Crusoe's devotion to his dog to a point at which almost any other filmmaker would have to cede utterly to sentimentality. Where Defoe has Crusoe describe his goat-skin outfits and comment "I could not but smile at the notion of my travelling through Yorkshire . . . in such a dress," Buñuel, following Defoe's details of Crusoe's attire very faithfully, presents to us a man whose clothes perfectly express the desperate eccentricity which alone carries him through his solitude. Even Crusoe's notorious difficulty with seeing Friday as anything but a slave is made to seem as if rather puzzling to Crusoe himself; we're permitted to laugh. Buñuel seems to allow for the possibility that we already understand all that is hateful in the Crusoe figure; what he asks us to discover is the power of loneliness to seduce a monster from his own evils. The remission of Crusoe's sins is, of course, only for a time, lasting a scant twenty-eight years before the man can gratefully embrace the bourgeois world once again, dressed to his station as Friday is dressed down to the station that will be his in civilized climates. But what counts is our sense of the cost of even temporary remission: in these areas, Buñuel knows, there are no bargains.

"I didn't like the novel but I liked the character" says Buñuel of Defoe's *Crusoe*. At first glance the thing is impossible. Crusoe and Crusoe's book are one; Defoe himself, in his various sequels, never came close to reanimating the organism of narrative and narrator that is the tale of Robinson on the island. But beneath Defoe's novel reposes another fiction, the myth he made when he made the novel, the most affecting modern myth of exile and seclusion; and it's the central figure of this myth who can be "liked" by the filmmaker who understands exile as his own inescapable condition. And Buñuel helps himself to more than the mere bones of the myth. One isn't belying Defoe's book beyond recognition to describe it as the story of a man quarantined, apparently for life, with nature, the word of God, and the terror of death, until he is joined by another man—cannibal, libertine, black—whom he is free to love only in the name of humanity: which of Buñuel's original scenarios speaks more immediately to his own concerns?

And in still another sense Buñuel's *Robinson Crusoe*, now experienced for the first time in the frame of a retrospective, speaks to us as one of the most personal of all Buñuel's movies. Defoe tells of a man far from his natural soil who works at his artifacts. Some are triumphs, some flawed, some even absurd because of the man's own limitations and the tools at his disposal, but no matter: together the artifacts compose the visible record of a bottomless refusal to give up. This is Crusoe on his island; and this is Buñuel in Mexico, responsible for *Gran casino* and *El gran calavera* but then for *Los olvidados*, for *Una mujer sin amor* and *La hija del engaño* but also for *Robinson Crusoe*. ⬤

Victor Giudice

Translated with an Introduction by

ELIZABETH LOWE

Victor Giudice, resident of Rio de Janeiro, was recently singled out as one of Brazil's most significant "new" writers. His published works include numerous short stories, articles of literary criticism in major Brazilian publications and *Necrológio* (Rio de Janeiro: Edições O Cruzeiro, 1972), a collection of short stories. The author is now working on another volume of stories and a novel. Giudice works at the Banco do Brasil in Rio and teaches literature on the university level. His many other interests include music (he plays five instruments), photography and graphic design.

For Giudice, "fiction seems absurd because it is reality stripped of all its lies." *Necrológio* is marked by extraordinary verbal inventiveness, giving new dimensions to the tradition of experimental avant-garde prose that has unfolded through several generations of Brazilian Modernists since 1922. Giudice does not, however, sacrifice lucidity or incisiveness. The precision of his narrative structures, as carefully composed as a sonnet or a symphony, meticulously accentuates the unbridled anguish of his protagonists. His major themes are death and time, skillfully interwoven to achieve a philosophical resonance for which he has been compared in stature to Jorge Luis Borges. Subtle handling of the relationships between man and woman give a rich texture to these two dominant themes.

Giudice interjects sly social criticism that goes beyond the local to an ironic attitude towards human behavior. He writes urban fiction, dwelling on the no-exit predicament of industrial man, regardless of social status. Giudice is especially resourceful in altering our perceptions of the commonplace and inverting "normal" relationships, such as that of life and death. Some of his stories branch into the marvelous.

Giudice's work has been published in Spanish translation in Argentina and Mexico. The following stories, all from *Necrológio*, are among the first English translations of his work.

ELIZABETH LOWE has recently completed a study entitled "The Urban Tradition in Brazilian Literature and the City in the Contemporary Brazilian Narrative."

The Pilgrimage of Old Auridéa

> Thus, when you give alms,
> sound no trumpet before you,
> as the hypocrites do in the
> synagogues and in the streets,
> that they may be praised by men.
> Truly, I say to you, they have
> their reward.
>
> Matthew, 6, 2

And, since everything was clear, and his knees did not have the same energy they used to, nor the same faith in the hilly streets, Bartholomew sat down on the first stoop of the stairway in front of the Cathedral and held out his hat to public charity.

(in the name of bread of the cold of the hunger I feel amen)

The evening before, there was fried swallow sprinkled with sauba ants, but winter arrived at midnight purpling the nails of the world, stones of the street, whistling silences, putting soft-breasted birds into flight.

Bartholomew smoked twisted straw, his nose in the warmth of the ember, until day returned. It returned: the sun was a brighter moon.

He looked at the church, the mist in the park, the park in the mist.

(the mist took away the park)

It took the trees, the lampposts, the people who did not go by, the lights of the dead houses.

And, since it also took away the shame, Bartholomew sat on the first stoop of the stairs in front of the Cathedral and held out his hat to public charity.

(in the name of bread, of the cold, of the hunger I feel amen)

The false day rose slowly, awakening mouldy overcoats, mufflers, wool socks, chamois boots and hurried gloves that frightened away the mist.

The moisture made the felt cold, obliging Bartholomew to change it from hand to hand every few moments so as not to freeze his fingers.

The hat, empty.

For a little while. Someone approaching making the sign of the cross: faith and the poor man.

(in the name of bread of the co)

The coin tumbled down from the air and Bartholomew felt the shock in the deep ex-emptiness.

The woman dragged her white shoes on the sidewalk, crossed herself again, dragged her white shoes, made another sign of the, dragged her shoes, made another, dragged, other, dragother, ragother, ragged, ragged.

Bartholomew saw the old woman disappear around the last corner, three blocks ahead, right in the middle of sign of the cross.

(heavy coin)

The brim bent under the sudden weight.

(funny)

He thought of putting the alms in his pocket, but the hat bent a little more.

He looked down at the coin and his pupils floated in fright: it was bigger.

(it grew)

The diameter the same as a match stick and five minutes later, the size of a cigarette.

Bartholomew left his courage on the first step of the stairway in front of the Cathedral and trembled in the middle of the park.

The children were laughing.

Bartholomew showed the phenomenon, its weight increasing still another time.

The pedestrians tripped on Bartholomew's fear and on the children's laughter. A man ordered one of them to call Sideral Smoke.

In an instant, the Cathedral Square was boiling in jeers and hoarse curses, while the curious formed a frightened circle around an old man with a yellow beard and a red jacket; Sideral Smoke, the demoralized sorcerer on account of successive failures in promises of rain.

Finally, Sideral wagged his beard, provoking a debauched silence.

—What's happening?

And his eyes squinted in the direction of the strange coin, already bigger than a saucer.

He took the money, examined it, smelled it, considered the weight, switching it from hand to hand and concluded:

—Copper.

The people mocked laughing:

—Copper.

Smoke reeled a threatening arm and faced Bartholomew:

—Who gave you this charity?

—She had white shoes, dragged her feet, and crossed herself.

The sorcerer scratched his beard, returned the coin and threw victories to the multitude:

—Auridéa. The coin is enchanted.

The catcalls did not succeed in shaking Sideral Smoke, his face pointed to the clouds.

—Another pilgrimage of Old Auridéa. It's always like that. It starts at the Cathedral and finishes at the Holy Virgin of the Spilled Blood. There are thirteen churches along the way. How many times has the weight increased?

Bartholomew did not understand:

—About four or five.

Now, it was the yellow beard that trembled.

—Go, my son. Take the south road. Only that way will you get to the Spilled Blood before she does. Auridéa is like lightning in those shoes. She will pass by the Bloodied Cross, by Our Lord of the Credited Afflictions, by the Martyr Dolorosa of the Lost Tear, by the Most Holy Virgin of the Immaculate Knoll, by the Most Beloved Mother of the Revealed Mystery, by the Seven Miracles of the Nails of Christ and by our Lady of Holy Despair. Nevertheless, she should not cross the Spilled Blood before you do. At every church you pass, the coin will grow heavier and larger, until it can no longer belong to you.

He spoke no more, turned on his heel, and opened way for himself through guffaws and fears.

Bartholomew did not hesitate. He put the coin into a burlap sack and his legs on to the south road.

He had not walked a hundred meters and the copper became a kilo heavier.

(MERCIFUL MOTHER OF THE BLOODIED CROSS)

Night came spreading frost on the highways. Bartholomew heard his stomach moan and caught sight of the dimmed lights of the city.

The weight doubled.

(OUR LORD OF THE CREDITED AFFLICTIONS)

He dragged the burden along the ground and felt like throwing himself into the dewy underbrush to wait for death, but he was aroused by a tremendous jolt.

MarTyr dOLOrOSA oF The LoST TEar)

The burlap jerked violently. Auridéa's little coin was a slice of the world.

(MOST hOLY virGIN of the imMAculATe KnOLL)

Bartholomew felt his feet moist with blood, but there was no pain. He fell for the first time.

(most beloved mother of the ReveAled myStEry)

He fell a second time.

(seven miracles of the nails of cHrist)

And he fell a third time.

(our lady of holy despair and MY OWN)

It was the last church before the Spilled Blood.

On the horizon, the mooned sun started to resuscitate and, from the side of darkness, Bartholomew guessed the black tower of the Mother Church of the Sacred Virgin of the Spilled Blood.

There, salvation.

He gained hidden strength.

(only a few more meters)

He arrived. Almost a corpse. But he arrived. He breathed deeply.

The coin had not suffered any transformation since Our Lady of Holy Despair, therefore, Auridéa was near.

And before he caught his breath, he noticed a dragging of soles coming steadily closer.

He tensed, his left hand on the mouth of the sack, the right on the handle of the knife he used to feather swallows.

He waited for Auridéa to reach him and introduced himself.

—I am the poor man of the Cathedral Stairs, to whom you gave an enchanted coin as alms.

Auridéa did not answer. She only let escape a long and thin grunt, while the blade tore her heart, difficult, between dry bones.

Finally, she stretched out on the stones of the sidewalk, her shoes dirty with rusty spots. Her eyes stayed open, lost among gray wrinkles.

Bartholomew trembled when he saw the coin shrink, shrink until it become a coin again.

He stuck it in his pocket and returned.

During the journey, he spent the money on coffee and buttered bread.

And, as everything returned to the before and winter had put the soft-breasted birds into flight, Bartholomew sat down on the first step of the Cathedral stairway and held out his hat to public charity.

(in the name of bread of the cold of the hunger I feel amen)

The hurried gloves frightened the mist from the park.

Bartholomew dozed distracted and something woke him up, when it hit the frozen felt.

He looked. It was another coin. Yellow as the beard of the demoralized sorcerer. Yellow and shining.

—GOOOOOOOOOOOOOOOLLLLLLLLLDDD.

The shout clanged in the Cathedral bels.

He was going to thank the charity, but he saw an old woman walking away making signs of the cross and dragging white shoes with little rust spots.

Bartholomew began to feel the coin shrink in his clenched hands.

He pressed what was left of the gold between his fingers

(in the name of bread of the cold of the hunger I feel) got up and went to call Sideral Smoke.

(amen)

In Perpetuum

get through another night: peacefully.

Is it always like that?

Always.

The bell never rings?

Never.

Because before six, Debi Mediocriz unsleeps the badly slept, turns off the alarm clock and repeats himself in bed, breathing deepnesses. He waits for the sharp thing to answer in his chest. It answers: a taste of the night before in his mouth. From his mouth to yesterday's paper. From his bed to yesterday's chair, picking up yesterday's clothes, going to yesterday's bathroom, urinating yesterday's urine, washing yesterday's face, brushing yesterday's teeth, combing yesterday's hair, going back into yesterday's room, putting away his pajamas.

(yesterday's)

The landlady yesterdays herself in goodbyes without deyesterdaying the days' work.

The waiter continues the exchange of obscenities with the worker.

And Debi?

Debi? Holds a cup of coffeemilk and a piece of bread and butter in suspension.

Nothing else?

Plus a pack of cigarettes and a box of matches.

Debi eats without hurry. Eyes lowered, on the way to the bus stop, smoking his first cigarette.

First?

Of the day. He waits for the bus, stands the whole way, hands on the rail, reading a magazine over the seated passenger's shoulder.

But he only got off two years later. In the center of the city, walking for five minutes at a calm pace until he arrived at the bank, a grey building with gold doors.

What for?

To punch in, to put away his blue shirt in the closet, to put on a yellowed shirt, to bind his neck in a brown clip-on bow tie, to wave at his waving colleagues, to sit down at work, to take out of the drawer a pile of white cards, to meditate over a sheet of paper with numbers printed on it, to

—How's it going, Debi? Did you find the discrepancy?

                        hear the question of the boss and let three years go by before answering:

—Not yet.

—Not yet?

—Not yet.

—Then get on it. See if you can finish this up before the man comes in.

Debi Mediocriz continued to study the cards with two waits too many: the manager and the colleague who shares his work table who

   (never arrives on time)

was also the colleague in the discrepancy.

Finally, he arrived. Debi said goodmorning and gave him the numbered sheet:

—The difference.

—If I could, I would pay it out of my own pocket.

—But you can't. Shoot.

The clerk droned his sums in a monochordous

(like the Mass for the Dead)

                                            voice.

—three thousand four hundred and twenty-nine and thirty-five and two million two hundred and twenty-three thousand nine hundred and fifteen and eighty

Mediocriz made little checks beside the numbers.

            six million three hundred and forty and eight thousand six hundred and thirty-four and ten nine million two hundred and fifty and nine thousand one hundred and sixteen and sixty

—Sixty or seventy?

—Six-oh.

The co-worker smiled a hope, but Debi shrugged his shoulders:

—Right. Go on.

—   two thousand twenty-seven and forty-eight and seven million four hundred and ninety-six one thousand five hundred and fifty-nine and thirty-two.

As soon as five years were over, Debi Mediocriz interrupted the meeting and said to the boss:

—Still nothing. Can we go to lunch?

—Go ahead. But finish this up. The man is furious. After lunch the thing has to show up.

It was time to wait for the ham and cheese sandwich, a boiled egg and a beer. He waited and ate. He paid and returned to the bank at the usual pace, smoking another cigarette misspending pupils in installment-plan showcases.

When he breathed deeply and the thing answered in his chest, Debi spit on the sidewalk.

Why?

Because the colleague started up again:

—six million four hundred and forty-two one thousand three hundred
and twenty-seven and ninety-seven thousand two hundred and sixty-
nine and sixteen eleven million five hundred and twenty-three thousand
seven hundred and thirty-four and forty

—Just a minute. The point of the pencil broke.

Debi Mediocriz unwrapped a rusty blade, sharpened another point
and wiped the shine off his brow with the back of his hand.

At two twenty there was a break: the boss authorized Debi to go to
the washroom:

—But see that you get right back here and find the discrepancy. The
man is complaining.

Debi sat in the bathroom with his legs stretched out over the passing
minutes.

He breathed.

New answer.

Another spit.

(hell: I'll have to get myself checked)

Then, he wiped himself, pulled up his pants and returned to the
seven million eight hundred and thirty-four one thousand two hundred
and twenty-five two million fourhun

Twelve years later, at seven thirty at night, Debi Mediocriz stopped
work, under the interrogation of the boss. He looked away:

Unfortunately, it has still not been possible.

—Really. I don't know what I am going to tell the man. Wait here.
Did Debi wait?

He waited. The passage of time without meaning or direction. Standing. He waited for the door to open, to close, to open. He waited for the
boss' face to leave the main office, approach and close as he closed the
door:

—You're lucky that the man's already left. See if you can finish to-
morrow. He's already fuming.

Debi Mediocriz excused himself and left.

What for?

To put away the yellow shirt and clip-on brown bow tie, to put on
the blue shirt, to leave, to buy the paper, to get in the bus line to wait.

The bus came. Another trip, other hands on the rail, reading another
magazine over the shoulder of another seated passenger.

To the boarding house?

To the boarding house.

And then?

Take a bath, shave, go out, isolate himself in a bar, ask for a beer
and drink slowly. Smoking his distance from the conversation at other
tables: the same ones as usual. Smoking and waiting.

For what?

For the clock to read ten forty. Then, he returned to his room, put on
his pajamas, set the alarm clock for six. He lay down, looked at the
headlines and lit up a cigarette.

The last?

Of the day. In an instant, the newspaper fell on the floor, since some-
body was whistling an unfamiliar tune, sleep did not come and the
news was yesterday's.

Debi Mediocriz closed his eyes and waited two more years, (tomor-

row the discrepancy will show up)
   And that way he was able
   Was he?

                               to get through another night: peacefully.
   Nevertheless, before six, Debi Mediocriz unsleeps the badly slept and turns off the alarm.
   The bell never rang?
   Never.
   Is it always like that?
   Always.

Death, Agony and Life of F.

On the day of his death, the doctors looked at F.'s eyes and disexchanged glances: F. had died with one kilo on his frog's face and three hundred and twenty grams in wrinkles of varying tones from yellow to purple to win the hearts of the nurses in Public Maternity.

There was no need to cut the umbilical cord, since the aforementioned cord did not resist the wrench of death and severed itself in the rapid confusion of the world with some other dirty trick.

While this was going on, the camel tried unceasingly.

Twenty-four hours later, F. was still dying and Science did not become alarmed because the death of Fs do not scare a dying soul. Nevertheless, F. was dying and perhaps would continue to die ad aeternitatem.

When he was five years dead, F. had a mother in a hilarious conjunction of two vehicles. The distinguished lady dirties clothes to guarantee the surdyval of F. and herself. She balanced herself on top of a bundle of clean clothes, at the exact moment that the drivers were waving to each other.

F. went to an orphanage and on Saturdays tortured himself with one or another goody thrown to him by the fathers and mothers of the orphans.

Earlier, he was transferred to a French perfume factory, becoming an almost brilliant worker due to his idea of adding a few drops of sulphuric acid to the flasks.

The commercial success resulting from such a practice was so unmistakable that the director-president of the firm, in a rare moment of euphoria, fired F., committing suicide immediately thereafter.

The episode brought pleasant consequences and F. was obliged to spend some time at the expense of the State, under the protection of distinguished gentlemen, whose good taste was evident in their habit of dressing in identical clothes.

At noon, F. devoured his gruel with such gusto that he turned down dinner.

Thus, F.'s death was punctuated by successive glories until he met Auriflor. When they saw each other, they cried inconsolably and exchanged a profound hate. They beat and bit each other in the most well lit corners.

The camel tried again, did not succeed, got its second wind, and carried on.

Auriflor and F., coerced by the superficiality of a millenial reflection, decided to die together until life should part them.

At that time, F. was suffering an enviable financial situation: he had applied himself to the study of Numerology, publishing an article in the Revue de Sciences Mathématiques of the University of Pará. He was selected as one of the probable losers of the Nobel Prize. Then, to disprove his own thesis, he stole a ticket. The Lottery won. F. received kudos from the whole world when he paid the prize to the institution in one hundred and forty-four weekly installments without interest.

That was the fly in the ointment. Auriflor seeing herself filthy rich at the side of the only man she hated, abandoned him. She exchanged F. for some R.

F. emerged from the salutary depression in the measure of the speed with which he unpacked his bags, tore up his passport and flew to the fasting room. He did not get along badly there. He moved into the waking room. The anguish of happiness drove him to fifty, forty, thirty, twenty, despair. It was encouraging. Nothing made him remember the hated woman.

And the camel in another fruitless attempt.

F. enrolled in a stenography course, graduated in sewing and, in a competition for the position of sacristan in a literary church, was eliminated in the next to the last place. He returned to his old job and sank into lethargy in the search for memories. Happily, he was nominated for the job of lamppost. Despite his love for dogs, he wore himself out. He turned on at six and turned off an hour earlier. It was too little. He dedicated himself to crime: opened a dry goods store, wetting the merchandise. The clientele discovered the fraud and showered him with the basest praise. F. tolerated everything. The firm became a charity case. F. wasted the opportunity and bought shares. Ten million, twenty, thirty, fifty, ninety. When the shareholders became aware of the plot, they decorated themselves with one hundred sixty-nine Smith & Wessons and paid him a visit. F. did not suspect they were after him. He sat down on the curb to fondle the ninety million. The shareholders surrounded F. F. ran backwards. The shareholders in the opposite direction. Back. Forth. Back. Forth. Back. Forth. The forths closed in the circle. F. in the middle. Someone did a sleight of hand and pulled a tambourine out of his pocket. Imitations followed.

The camel tried again.

Thirty-eight shareholders formed a percussion band. Four ukeleles and twenty-one drums.

F. started to dance first. The shareholders followed suit.

The camel launched the last try.

The samba rhythm numbed the desert drowned in so much satisfaction. Always in the middle of the circle, F. whirled nonexistence on the tip of an invisible banner.

He danced until his skin began to glow with the same purplish-yellow as when he died. Then, he lay down on the ground, smiled in the memory of Auriflor, opened his eyes and lived.

But it was too late, the camel, after two thousand years of failure, finally succeeded in getting through the eye of the needle, and in so doing, there was no room for F.

Proyección cúbica. 1971. Object. 100 x 60 x 28 cm.

Felisberto Hernández

Translated with an Introduction by

LUIS HARSS

Felisberto Hernández (1902-1964) wrote very little. His early works—*Fulano de tal* (1925), *Libro sin tapas* (1929), *La cara de Ana* (1930), *La envenenada* (1931)—were mostly sketches and fragments that break off almost in mid-sentence. He liked to think of himself as suddenly "blinking" a scene into being and then dropping it as it inevitably faded in his mind. He worked hardest at waiting for things to come, then trying to hold them and finally registering the act of losing them. His *Libro sin tapas*, for instance, was an "open" book, blank (or unbound) at both ends. In a later story called "The Flooded House" we see him listening at doors that open silently on to sleeping figures whose thoughts, as he says, "are not mine but are meant for me." The theme of "stolen thoughts" becoming his own is a major part of his dream imagery. There is a moment when he realizes he has forever been storing "memories that don't belong to me." The memories come to him in "words that seemed to have been around in many mouths and reached me through very different voices, from distant times and places," claiming "a meaning I had never given them." He can suddenly hear them "ringing prophetically" inside him, as if transmitted by "a mouth speaking for this world, with eyes set beyond it." At moments he is "like an empty room, with even myself missing," at others "like a poor tavern in the middle of a fair." In the "Explicación falsa de mis cuentos," a sketch in his usual whimsical tone that could well be translated as "How I Don't Write My Stories," he speaks of the strangeness of the "plant" being born "in

LUIS HARSS, who teaches Spanish at the University of West Virginia, is the co-author of *Into the Mainstream.*

some corner of me," and his cautious waiting for it to bloom into "leaves of poetry or something that could become poetry when seen by certain eyes." He must tend and watch the plant without pushing or forcing it into a false beauty, allowing it to reach its own natural intensity, "unknown to itself." The enemy is consciousness, always threatening to intrude with its set ways. Each story has "it's own strange life"; and, in a memorable phrase from one of those stories, "I don't think I should say only what I know, but also the rest."

As it happens, Felisberto Hernández did not begin as a writer but as a pianist. At twelve he was accompanying silent movies in Montevideo; at twenty he was touring the smalltown circuit that provides the setting for so many of his stories. It was a lonely, desperate life—his "crying crocodile" period—of shabby theaters and dingy hotels. Typically his stories draw on the ghostly acquaintances he made during his concerts. Most are written in the first person. A kind of tinkling music accompanies them into their glimpses of madness and secret vice. A quiet, constant despair breaks through the childish humor. The dreamlike innocence often takes on erotic undertones. There is a sense of feeding on one's own misery. As a character says, fearing he may be cured of his obsession, "I love my illness more than life itself." There is the guilt and self-pity born of monstrous yearnings as "each day I write better and I feel worse." And always, there is the longing for "the lost horse of childhood," which becomes the central theme in *Por los tiempos de Clemente Colling* (1942), *El caballo perdido* (1943) and *Tierras de la memoria* (a posthumous work written in 1944). In these longer but still fragmentary works, as in the stories of *Nadie encendía las lámparas* (1947), the moving force is memory, which keeps breaking down. The rambling plot in "The Lost Horse"—like a tinkling piano tune losing a note—soon dissolves into the vagaries of memory itself. In "Lands Of Memory" an insect buzzes back and forth with the little dim lamp of the searching mind, like a thirsty animal "still in the habit of coming to drink at a spot where there was no more water."

As music became words in Felisberto Hernández, his life seemed to decay. We know of a grandmother who beat him; a mother who never let go and took him back after four broken marriages; his failure as a musician; his notebooks full of a mysterious personal shorthand that has not been deciphered; his slow spiritual death in miserable roominghouses; the six "widows" at his funeral.

In a sense he was a naïf: a man working beyond his means. Though he suffered and labored over his stories, sometimes for months, there is always something a bit rough about them. It used to be said that he wrote badly. But perhaps it would be fairer to say "inarticulately," in the sense that all poetry is inarticulate when it approaches the unsayable. He was superstitious about words and his doubtful "friendship" with them. In some, above all simple words, he found a "mysterious sympathy." Others he found unnatural or pretentious and he tried to avoid them, in complex ways. There is an instinctive critique of language in his work that has yet to be appreciated. And a lesson in humility to be learned from his lonely search for those "nooks, rhythms and turns of speech" that lead beyond words.

A Windy Morning

On a windy morning my parents took me to a drugstore. I was eleven years old. The druggist was a friend of the family and my parents told him I was weak. He made me stick my tongue out and then had a long talk with them. While no one was looking, I went and stuck my tongue out between two mirrors that faced each other. I saw myself and my tongue multiplied many times, my farthest "selves" rising in the distance toward the ceiling—the mirrors were tilted forward, as if bowing at each other—till finally only my feet were visible.

The next morning there was sun. My father got the buggy hitched up early and we left for the country. After a while I was bored and I fell asleep. At noon we came to a small town where there was a tin shed with my name and surname painted on it in big letters, and underneath the words: "Snacks 'round the clock." My father laughed and said I and the owner of the shed were the only ones in the whole country with the same name and surname.

Inside the shed there were round tables, as at the beach, and a man in shirtsleeves sent the waiter over to take our order. My father asked for steaks with french fries and fried eggs. The waiter passed the order on to a lady behind the counter who stuck her head through a hole in a partition to send it on to someone on the other side. We were the only customers. In a while the man in shirtsleeves came up to the table and my father asked him if he was the owner and told him that he and I had the same name, and they both laughed. But I felt miserable.

The owner spoke through his carefully curled black mustache. His forelock was also curled, like another mustache. He picked his teeth with a straw from a broom and had a little finger with a long nail. I had lost all confidence in myself: I might be that man or anyone else. When I wrote my grandmother, instead of signing my name I'd send her my picture, and when thinking of myself I'd look in the mirror.

But then I remembered all the "selves" I'd seen in the mirrors the day before and saw them again sticking their tongues out.

The Balcony

There was a town I liked to visit in summer. It had a neighborhood that just about emptied at that time of the year when people left for a nearby resort. One of the empty houses was very old; it had been turned into a hotel, and as soon as summer came it looked sad and started to lose its best families, until only the servants remained. If I had hidden behind it and let out a shout, the moss would have swallowed it right up.

The theater where I was giving my concerts was also half empty and invaded by silence: I could see it growing on the big black top of the piano. The silence liked to listen to the music, to let it ring and then wait and think it over for a while before giving its opinion. But when it began to feel more at home it took part in the music. Then it was like a cat with a long black tail that slipped in between the notes and haunted them.

At the end of one of those concerts, a timid old man came up to shake my hand. The bags under his blue eyes looked sore and swollen. He had a huge lower lip that bulged out like the the edge of a theater box. He barely opened his mouth to speak, in a slow, dull voice, wheezing at each word.

After a long pause he said:

"I'm so sorry my daughter can't hear you play."

I don't know why it occurred to me that his daughter was blind; though at once I realized that would not have prevented her from hearing me, so that she was more likely deaf or perhaps out of town; which suddenly led to the idea that maybe she was dead. And yet I was happy that night. Everything in that town was quiet and slow as we walked, floating through greenish shadows.

Suddenly bending toward him, as if watching over something very brittle, I caught myself asking:

"Your daughter can't come?"

He let out a sharp "Ah"; stopped, looked into my face and finally managed to say:

"Yes, that's it. She can't go out. You understand. Sometimes she can't sleep nights thinking she has to go out the next day. In the morning she's up early, getting ready, working herself up to it. But it wears off after a while, she just drops into a chair. By then she can't go out any more."

The people leaving the concert soon disappeared from the streets around the theater and we went into a café. He called the waiter, who brought him a dark drink in a small glass. I was only going to spend a few minutes with him: I had to have dinner elsewhere. So I said:

"It's a shame she can't go out. We all need a bit of entertainment."

He raised the glass to his big lip, which didn't quite manage to touch the drink, and explained:

"She has her own way of keeping entertained. I bought an old house, too big for just the two of us, but it's in good shape. It has a garden with a fountain; and in a corner of her room there's a door that opens on a winter balcony; and the balcony faces the street. You could almost says she lives in that balcony. Or sometimes she goes for a walk in the garden and on some nights she plays the piano. You can come and have dinner with us whenever you want, I'd be grateful to you."

I understood at once; and so we agreed on a day when I would go for dinner and play the piano.

He called for me at the hotel one afternoon when the sun was still high. From a distance, he showed me the corner with the winter balcony. It was on a second floor. The entrance was through a large gate to one side of the house. It opened on to a garden with a fountain and some small statues hidden in the weeds. Around the garden ran a high wall. The top of the wall was all splintered glass stuck in mortar. A flight of steps led up into the house, through a glassed-in corridor from where one could see the garden. I was surprised to notice a lot of open parasols in the long corridor; they were of different colors and looked like huge hothouse plants. The old man hastened to explain:

"I gave her most of the parasols. She likes to keep them open to see the colors. When there's good weather she picks one and goes for a little walk in the garden. On windy days you can't open this door because the parasols blow away. We have to use another entrance."

We reached the far end of the corridor along the space left between the wall and the parasols. We came to a door and the old man rapped on the glass. A muffled voice answered from inside. The old man led me in and at once I saw his daughter standing in the center of the winter balcony, facing us, with her back to the colored panes. We were halfway across the room before she left the balcony and approached us. From far off she was already raising her hand and thanking me for my visit. Leaning against the darkest wall of the room was a small open piano. It looked innocent, with its big yellowish smile.

She excused herself for not being able to go out, and pointing to the balcony, said:

"He's my only friend."

I pointed to the piano and asked:

"How about this poor soul? Isn't he also your friend?"

We sat in chairs at the foot of her bed. I had time to notice many small paintings of flowers, all hung at the same height, along the four walls, as though parts of a frieze. She wore a forgotten smile as innocent as the piano's; but her faded blonde hair and wispy figure also seemed to have been long forgotten. She was starting to explain why the piano wasn't as much her friend as the balcony when the old man left almost on tiptoes. She went on saying:

"The piano was a great friend of my mother's."

I made as if to go over and look at it, but she raised a hand and opened her eyes wide to stop me.

"I'm sorry but I'd rather you tried the piano after dinner when the lights are on. Since I was a little girl I got into the habit of hearing the piano only at night. That was when my mother played it. She used to light the four candles in the candlesticks and play each note so slowly and distinctly in the stillness, it was as if she were also lighting up the sounds, one by one."

Then she rose and, excusing herself, went out on the balcony, where she leaned her bare arms on the panes as if she were resting them on someone's breast. But she came right back and said:

"When I see the same man go by several times through the red pane, he usually turns out to be violent or mean."

I couldn't help asking her:

"What pane did you see me through?"

"The green one. It usually means someone who lives alone in the country."

"I happen to like being alone among plants," I said.

The door opened and the old man came in followed by a maid who was so short that I couldn't tell whether she was a child or a dwarf. Her ruddy face shone over the little table she was carrying in her tiny arms. The old man asked me:

"What will you drink?"

I was going to say "Nothing"; but I thought that would offend him, so I asked for something or other. He had the maid bring him a small glass with the same dark drink I'd seen him take after the concert.

As night fell we started for the dining room. We had to go through the corridor of the parasols. The girl changed a few of them around and glowed when I praised them.

The dining room was below street level. Through the window gratings one could see the feet and legs of the people going by on the sidewalk. A lamp with a green shade poured its light straight on the white tablecloth. There, old family possessions had come together, as if remembering past times. As we sat, we were quiet for a moment; and then all the things on the table seemed to take on a deep silent meaning. Our pairs of hands started to appear on the tablecloth, as if they belonged there. I couldn't stop thinking of the life they gave things. Years back, hands had shaped and molded these objects on the table. After much handling, the plates, glasses and other small beings had found their home in a sideboard. Over the years they had had to serve all sorts of hands. Any one of those hands could pour food on the plates' smooth bright faces, could make the jars fill and empty their hips, the knives and forks sink into the meat and cut it up into pieces for eating. Finally the small beings were scrubbed, dried and led back to their little rooms. Some of these beings could survive many pairs of hands. Some of the hands would be kind to them, would love them and be long remembered; but the things would have to go on serving in silence.

A while back, when we were in the girl's bedroom and she had not yet turned on the light—she didn't want to miss the last glow from the balcony—we had spoken of the objects. As the light faded, they nestled in the shadows as if they had feathers and were preparing to sleep. She said they grew souls as they came in touch with people. Some had once been something else and had another soul (the ones with legs had once had branches, the piano keys had been teeth). But her balcony had first had a soul when she started to live in it.

Suddenly the ruddy face of the dwarf maid appeared over the rim of the tablecloth. Though she reached out firmly to grasp things in her tiny hands, the old man and his daughter slid their plates near the edge of the table for her. But when she took them, the objects on the table lost their dignity. The old man also had a hasty, tactless way of grabbing the jug by the neck and wringing the wine out of it.

At first conversation was difficult. Then a big grandfather clock started pounding out the time. It had been looming against the wall behind the old man, but I had forgotten its presence. Then we started to talk. The girl asked me:

"Aren't you fond of old clothes?"

"Of course! And according to what you said about objects, clothes are the ones that have been in the closest touch with us"—here I laughed and she remained serious—"and I wouldn't be surprised if they kept something more of us than just the unavoidable shapes of our bodies and a whiff of our skin."

But she wasn't listening. Instead, she had been trying to interrupt me, like someone waiting to skip over a flipping rope. No doubt she had asked me the question thinking of what she would have answered. Finally she said:

"I make up my poems in bed"—she had already mentioned those poems in the afternoon—"and I have a white nightgown that has been with me since my first poems. Some summer nights I wear it out on the balcony. Last year I wrote a poem to it."

She had stopped eating and didn't seem to notice the dwarf's arms coming and going. Staring as in a vision, she began to recite:

"To my white nightgown."

I strained to listen, at the same time watching the dwarf's hands. Her tiny, stubby fingers were clenched as they approached things. They unbent only at the last moment, to clasp them.

At first I tried to find different ways to show attention but then I just nodded, in time to the swinging motion of the clock's pendulum. This bothered me; and I also worried about the girl's finishing before I could think of anything to say. Besides, the old man had a bit of chard dangling from his lower lip near the corner of his mouth.

The poem was corny; but it seemed to have the right number of syllables. The rhymes were unexpected: I would tell her it was fresh. Watching the old man, I had passed my tongue over my lower lip; but he was listening to his daughter. Now I began to feel the poem was dragging on forever. Suddenly she joined "nightgown" and "balcony," and that was the end of it.

From the first words, I had been listening to myself calmly and giving the impression I was looking for something that I was on the point of finding.

"I'm struck by the childish quality of the poem," I began. "It's very fresh and . . ."

As I started to say "fresh" she also started to say:

"I have another . . ."

I felt miserable. I thought of myself with treacherous selfishness. The dwarf arrived with another platter and I made a show of helping myself generously. All the glamour was gone from the objects on the table, the poem, the house around me, even the parasols in the corridor and the ivy that grew up one whole side of the house. Worse, I felt cut off from them and ate shamelessly. There wasn't a time the old man clutched the neck of the jug that my glass wasn't empty.

When she finished her second poem, I said:

"If this wasn't so good"—and I nodded at my plate—"I'd ask for another."

The old man said at once:

"She should eat first. There'll be time for that later."

I was starting to feel cynical, and at that moment I wouldn't have minded growing a huge paunch. But suddenly I felt a sort of need to cling to the poor old man's jacket and be kind to him. So, pointing to the wine, I said I'd once heard a story about a drunkard. I told it and when it ended they both started to laugh desperately. So I told them more stories. There was sorrow in the girl's laugh; but she begged me to go on telling my stories. Her mouth had stretched at the edges, into a painful gash. Her frowning eyes were full of tears and she was pressing her clasped hands between her knees. The old man was coughing and had to put down the jug before filling his glass. The dwarf laughed bending as if to bow.

We had all been miraculously united, and I felt not the least regret.

That night I did not play the piano. They begged me to stay and led me to a bedroom on the side of the house where the ivy grew. As I started up the stairs, I noticed a cord that ran from the grandfather clock all the way up the winding staircase. I followed it into the bedroom, up to the canopied bed, where it ended tied to the bedpost. The room had ancient, yellowish furnishings with sagging bellies that shone in the lamplight. I put my hands on my stomach and watched to see what the old man would do. His last words that night were to suggest:

"If you can't sleep and want to know what time it is, pull on the cord. You'll hear the dining room clock from here. First it will give you the hour, then after a pause, the minutes."

Suddenly he began to laugh and went out waving goodnight. He was probably remembering one of the stories, the one about a drunkard who talked to a clock.

He was still making the wooden stairs creak with his heavy steps when I started to feel alone with my body. It had absorbed all that food and drink like an animal swallowing another animal, and now it would have to struggle with it all night long. I stripped it naked and made it go barefoot around the room.

Lying in bed, I tried to figure out what I was doing with my life those days. I fished a few recent events out of my memory and thought of some people who were very far away. Then, sadly and almost lewdly, I started to slide down something that was like a silent bowel.

The next morning I looked back over my life with an almost happy smile. It was very early. I dressed slowly and went out into a corridor built over the edge of the garden. On this side, too, there were weeds and tall shady trees. I heard the old man and his daughter talking and realized they were on a bench right underneath me. I caught her words first:

"Ursula is unhappier now. She not only loves her husband less, but loves someone else more."

The old man asked:

"Can't she get a divorce?"

"No, because she loves her children, and the children love her husband and not the other man."

Then the old man said timidly:

"She could tell the children that her husband has several mistresses."

She got up angrily:

"Just like you to say that! When will you understand Ursula? She would never say such a thing!"

I was very much intrigued. They couldn't be talking about the dwarf: her name was Tamarinda. According to what the old man had told me, they lived completely alone. So where did this news come from? Might it have reached them during the night? After her burst of anger, the girl had gone into the dining room, and in a while she came back out into the garden carrying a salmon-colored parasol with white gauze ruffles. She did not come to the table for lunch. The old man and I drank and ate little. Afterwards I went out to buy a book suitable for reading in an abandoned house among the weeds, on a still night and a full stomach.

On my way back, just ahead of me, I saw a poor old black man limp past the balcony. He wore a green hat with a wide brim, like a Mexican. Just then a spot of white skin appeared in the balcony, through the green pane.

That night, as soon as we sat down to eat, I started telling my stories, and she did not recite her poems.

The laughs the old man and I let out covered up for the brutal amounts of food and drink we were putting away.

There was a moment when we fell silent. Then the daughter said:

"I want to hear music tonight. I'll go in ahead of you and light the candles on the piano. It's been a long time since they were lit. The poor old piano will think it's Mother who's come to play."

Neither the old man nor I said another word. In a while Tamarinda came in to say the young lady was waiting for us.

When I was about to strike the first chord, the silence was like a heavy animal with a paw raised. The chord broke into rippling sounds like the wavering candlelight. I tried another chord, as if advancing another step. And almost at once, before I reached the next chord, a string snapped. The girl cried out. The old man and I jumped up. He bent over his daughter, who had her face in her hands, and tried to calm her, telling her the strings were old and rusted. But she wouldn't take her hands off her face or stop shaking her head. I didn't know what to do; I'd never snapped a string before. I asked to be excused; and on the way to my room I was afraid of stepping on the parasols in the corridor.

The next morning I missed most of the conversation on the garden bench; but I was in time to hear the girl say:

"Ursula's love came wearing a big green hat with a huge wide brim."

I couldn't believe she meant the old black man I had seen limping by the previous afternoon; nor could I imagine who might have brought the news during the night.

At noon the old man and I had lunch alone again. It was my chance to say:

"There's a lovely view from the corridor. I would have stayed there longer but I heard you talking about a certain Ursula and I was afraid to intrude."

The old man stopped eating and whispered:

"You heard us?"

I saw he wanted to confide in me, and answered:

"Yes, everything. But I don't see how Ursula can find that old black man handsome, with his limp and his wide green hat."

"Oh, but you haven't understood," he said. "Since my daughter was hardly more than a child she's been making me listen to her stories and take part in the lives of the characters she invents. And since then we've been keeping track of them as if they really existed and we kept hearing from them. She imagines them wearing and doing things she sees from the balcony. If yesterday she saw a man in a green hat go by, it's not surprising the hat turned up today on one of her characters. I'm too clumsy to keep up with her, and she gets angry with me. Why don't you help her? If you want I'll . . ."

I didn't let him finish.

"I wouldn't think of it. I'd only invent things that would hurt her."

That evening, too, she was absent from the table. The old man and I ate, drank and chatted until well into the night.

Later, in bed, I heard a board creak somewhere outside the room. After a while I realized it was someone coming up the stairs. And soon there was a soft rap on my door. I asked who it was, and the girl's voice answered:

"It's me. I want to talk to you."

I switched on the lamp and opened the door a crack, and she said:

"It's no use hiding. I can see you in the mirror, standing there behind the door without a stitch on."

So I shut it and asked her to wait.

When I let her in she walked straight across the room to another door I had never been able to open. She opened it with the greatest ease and groped her way into the darkness of another room where I had never been. She came right back out with a chair that she placed by my bed. She reached into a blue cape she was wearing and took out a notebook, and started to read poems from it. I had to make a great effort not to fall asleep. I tried to keep my eyes open, but instead all I could do was roll them back, so that I must have looked like I was dying. Suddenly she cried out, as when the piano string had snapped, and I jumped in bed. There was a huge spider in the middle of the floor. By the time I saw it it was no longer moving: it had gathered up three of its hairy legs, as if ready to pounce. I threw my shoes at it and missed. I got up, but she told me to stay away or it would jump at me. So I took my lamp and edged along the walls, all the way around the room to the washbasin, from where I threw a brush, a cake of soap and my soap case. The case finally hit it, and it rolled up into a dark woolly ball. She asked me not to tell her father, who didn't like her to be up working or reading so late. When she left, I squashed the spider with my shoe and went back to bed without turning out the light. As I was about to fall asleep, I felt my toes curl. I thought the spider was in bed with me and I jumped up again.

In the morning the old man came in to apologize for the spider. His daughter had told him everything. I said it was nothing to worry about, and to change the subject I spoke of a concert I was about to give in a nearby town. He thought it was a pretext for leaving and I had to promise to return after the concert.

As we parted, I couldn't stop the girl from kissing my hand. I didn't know what to do. The old man hugged me, and suddenly I felt him kiss me near my ear.

I never got to my concert. A couple of days later I received a phone call from the old man. After the first few words he said:

"You have to come back."

"Has something serious happened?"

"I'd say a real tragedy."

"To your daughter?"

"No."

"To Tamarinda?"

"No, no. I can't tell you now. If you can postpone the concert, catch the four o'clock train and I'll meet you at the Theater Café."

"But your daughter is all right?"

"She's in bed. Not ill, but she doesn't want to get up or see the light of day. She can only stand lamplight and has had all the parasols folded."

"All right, I'll be there."

The Theater Café was too noisy, so we moved elsewhere.

The old man was depressed, but he cheered up at the sight of me. He ordered his dark drink in the usual little glass and said:

"The day before yesterday there was a storm. We were sitting in the dining room in the evening when we heard a big clatter. We realized at once it wasn't the storm. My daughter ran into her room and I followed her. When I got there she had already opened the door to the balcony, and all she saw was the sky and the light of the storm. She covered her eyes and fainted."

"So the light hurt her?"

"But, my God! Don't you understand?"

"What?"

"That we've lost the balcony. It fell out. It wasn't the balcony light she saw."

"But a balcony . . ."

It was better to say nothing. He made me promise not to mention the subject to the girl. So what was I to do? The poor old man was counting on me. I remembered the orgies we'd had together. And I decided to just wait and hope I could think of something when I saw her.

It was frightening to see the corridor without the parasols.

That night we ate and drank little. Then I accompanied the old man to his daughter's bedside, and he at once left the room. She hadn't said a word; but as soon as he was gone she turned toward the door that opened into space and said:

"You see how he left us?"

"But, I don't . . . A balcony that falls out . . ."

"He didn't fall. He jumped."

"All right, but . . ."

"Not only did I love him, but he also loved me. I know, because he'd already proved it."

I hung my head. I felt involved in an act of responsibility that I was not prepared for. She had started to pour her soul out and I didn't know how to receive it or what to do with it.

Now the poor girl was saying:

"It was all my fault. He got jealous the night I went to your room."

"You mean . . .?"

"Who do you think I mean? The balcony, my balcony."

"Now, isn't that making too much of it? Remember how old he was. There are things that fall of their own weight."

She wasn't listening. She went on:

"That same night I understood the warning and the threat."

"Now, come on. You don't mean to say . . ."

"Don't you remember who threatened me? Who stared and stared at me, twitching those three hairy legs?"

"Yes, of course! The spider!"

"It's all so much like him."

She looked up at me. Then she threw off the covers and got out of bed in her nightgown. She was headed for the balcony door and I thought she was going to jump out. I started to reach for her; but she was in her nightgown. While I hesitated, she corrected her course. Now she was going toward a little table next to the door that opened into space. On the little table, just before she reached it, I saw the notebook with the black oilcloth covers from which she read her poems.

She sat in a chair, opened the notebook and started to recite:

"The widow of the balcony . . ."

Just Before Falling Asleep

Often, just before falling asleep, I've remembered my family, as if blinking through a tiny hole I could light them up in my backyard. It was noon and I was returning from a city in the provinces and they hadn't seen me yet. They were gathered around a table set under the trees and I knew the patterns of light and shade on the tablecloth and how they combined each time the leaves moved in the breeze. Caught up in their small meals and their bit of happiness, they seemed oblivious to me. One night the memory recurred, like a self-repeating mechanism: again and again, they sat at the table and seemed oblivious to me. Suddenly the mechanism would stop, and then it would occur to me that those heads bent over the plates were somehow aware of my existence and carried that awareness around with them in a way that was probably very different from the way one carries around the awareness of a dead person. In any case I knew how my absence felt to them, and what they were like when they remembered me. But I also knew something else: that as I opened the door noiselessly that day and watched them through some reeds, I was already seeing them as if I were remembering them, and I already knew the memory would follow me. And I decided that if some day I had to survive them, that was how I would remember them, a bit at a distance and in silence. Sometimes the memory has followed me and caught up with me at night, and though the colors of the day were like those of an ordinary postcard, I could still see them smile.

Jaime Sabines in Translation

AMEEN ALWAN

Sabines is a tall, big-boned man. Born in southern Mexico (Chiapas) in 1925, he came to Mexico City to study medicine, but after two years shifted his studies to Spanish literature. While still at the university, he published his first two books: *Horal* (1950) and *La señal* (1951). In his middle twenties, Sabines had found his own voice, his own way of doing things so that the poetry in those books—especially in *La señal*—is characteristic of his later work. And much of that work has appeared as prose poetry. In fact, two of his books are made up entirely of prose poems: *Adán y Eva* (1952) and *Diario Semanario* (1961).

Sabines is essentially an urban poet whose work is suffused with a harsh or dark way of looking at things, a sense of alienation, pain. When a lyricism comes into his work, it enters against that background of pain, so it seems well-earned. There's an emphasis on relationships—particularly with his father—and also upon himself as a poet who exists in the world of jobs and employment. And, of course, his poetry tends to be autobiographical.

AMEEN ALWAN's poetry and translations of Latin American poets have appeared in many journals, including *The Paris Review*, *The Nation* and *Chelsea*.

In the spring of 1977 Joaquín Mortiz will publish a new edition of Sabines' collected poems, *Nuevo recuento de poemas,* which I am translating into English. The volume will include all his books except his last, *Maltiempo* (1972).

Perhaps a few words should be said about the method used in preparing the translation.

My main concern is that the poems work strongly in English. If they can be translated accurately and work well in English—that's the way I've done them.

A second group is made up of adaptations or versions. These are poems with many strong things in them, but presenting serious difficulties for translation, such as material that worked in Spanish but not in English.

The adaptations are of two sorts. The larger group mainly involves cuts. Then there are a few poems which I've rewritten in English, following a core that I think is strong in Spanish. The two poems printed here illustrate the adaptations.

In accordance with an agreement between Sabines and myself, the translations will be published bilingually, perhaps with literal translations for the adaptations at the foot of the Spanish.

MI CAMA ES DE MADERA

Mi cama es de madera
y cruje bajo el peso del amor jadeante,
pero mi cama es un barco inmóvil
que me lleva a donde quiero ir.
Carga mi soledad mejor que yo mismo
y conoce mis sueños
y se compadece de mí.
Mi cama es casi una nube,
es una alfombra para las pisadas de
                    mi corazón.

A media luz, o a obscuras,
en mi cama encuentro a mi mujer, mis hijos,
                    mis libros,

mis recuerdos y mis cigarros.
Y encuentro a Dios, a veces,
en la luz de una tarde como ésta,
que besa con la yema de sus dedos los
                    párpados cerrados.

Amo mi cama porque en ella reposo como en
                    mi muerte
y en ella siento que la vida puede ganarse
                    aún.

Estoy agradecido porque tengo una cama
y es lo mismo que si tuviera un río,
lo mismo.

A BOAT A CLOUD A CARPET
After "Mi cama es de madera"

my bed
is made of wood

a motionless

boat
it carries my solitude
better than myself

my bed
is almost a cloud

a carpet

for my heart's
footsteps

there

in the half light
I find

my wife
my children my books
memories cigarettes

I am pleased

it's the same

as if
I had a river

the same

EN LA ORILLA DEL AIRE

LOOK CAREFULLY
After "En la orilla del aire"

En la orilla del aire
(¿qué decir, qué hacer?)
hay todavía una mujer.

En el monte, extendida
Sobre la yerba,
si buscamos bien:
una mujer.

Bajo el agua, en el agua,
abre, enciende los ojos,
mírala bien.

Algas, ramas de peces,
ojos de náufragos,
flautas de té,
le cantan, la miran bien.

En las minas, perdida,
delgada, sombra también
raíces de plata obscura
le dan de beber.

A tu espalda, en donde estés,
si vuelves rápido a ver
la ves.
En el aire hay siempre oculta
como una hoja en un árbol
una mujer.

there's a woman
at

the air's edge

on the hill, stretched
over the grass

below the water
in the water

algae
branches of fish
tea flutes/
they sing to her

lost
in the mines

veins
of dark silver
give

her a drink

behind you
where you are
if you turn quickly
to see

you'll see her

hidden
in the air

like a leaf
in a tree

The Sanskrit Everyone Knows

Sacred Families: Three Novellas
By José Donoso
Translated by Andrée Conrad
Alfred A. Knopf, 1977. $7.95

Charleston and Other Stories
By José Donoso
Translated by Andrée Conrad
David R. Godine, 1977. $8.95

The Boom in Spanish American Literature:
A Personal History
By José Donoso
Translated by Gregory Kolovakos
Columbia University Press, 1977.
$9.00 (hardcover); $4.95 (paper)

PAUL WEST

With these three new books José Donoso doubles his published output to six, and the entertaining prospect suggests itself of a career that is either bumper crops or nothing, and of critical review as an act of the combined harvester. The truth, no doubt, is less spectacular: translators and publishers are only just catching up with Donoso, the Princeton-educated Chilean novelist now living outside Barcelona, fifty-three years old and (if *Sacred Families* is any indication) getting better—subtler, suppler, defter, craftlier—all the time. To some extent, it's unfortunate that three books arrive all at once; a longer hiatus than usual is bound to follow, and the man's continuing presence will not be felt except by those re-

PAUL WEST received *The Paris Review*'s Aga Khan Prize for Fiction in 1974; his eighth novel, *Gala,* was published recently by Harper and Row.

reading him, especially in a country that treats all of a novelist's novels as if they were first novels (as if he/she had not existed previously and were 'unlikely to survive past the present book). One can, however, clarify what kind of a writer Donoso is, discovering in him qualities not blatant in, say, *This Sunday* or *The Obscene Bird of Night:* in other words, adding to the almost philatelical skills of the documentary artist, and the half-Faulknerian atavist, something out of Ovid, the Ovid who, in his first despair at being banished to the Black Sea, burned his newly completed *Metamorphoses* (though the book was later rewritten from other copies), the Ovid who specialized in transformations and transmogrifications, all the way from Chaos to the apotheosis of Caesar. And as well as Ovid another auspex: Maurice Ravel, whose *Gaspard de la Nuit* gives its title to the last one of the *Tres novelitas burguesas* rather oddly revamped into "Sacred Families." It was Ravel who would suddenly interrupt a serious conversation by tilting his head to one side and letting out a bird cry, or who would mimic a seasick Chinese by covering an orange with a napkin and then squeezing it.

In other words, as well as once again Donoso the observing precisian (as well as Donoso Atavist), we have here a playful master of sleight of hand, an illusionist who, at his most forceful, is given to patient and energetic scrutinies of the mental set that underlies each act of phenomenology, and, at his most languid, arranges successive takes of an object, a person, in bewitching left-to-right notations that have eidetically the impact of spirals. It isn't quite enough to say, as one piece of flap copy does, that "all is not what it seems"; all indeed *is* what it seems, and *all* that it seems, and almost non-stop in the three novellas. There is no gamut (gamut has a limit), but an implied infinity of changes that obtains for as long as there are perceivers who think there is something outside themselves they are working on. And even then, even if there are perceivers only, unable to communicate with one another, the noetic conjuring goes on, shuttling back and forth between Coleridge's primary and secondary imaginations, doodling until the synesthetic void fills up (like the youth in "Gaspard de la Nuit" who whistles in private orchestration of his loneliness). Six years ago, in an interview appended to my novel *Caliban's Filibuster* to complicate rather than sweeten the pill, I told George Plimpton that "If someone thinks he is there in Australia with aborigines being maltreated and circumcized and crucified and God knows what . . . then, he is." I still think so: if it's real for you it's real for you, and if you don't comport yourself mentally as if it is real for you, you're stuck.

Hence my sympathy with Donoso's three novellas, which compose the best book of these three. Not only does he create in intricate, copious résumés the material clutter of his chosen bourgeois (doctor, dentist, model), defining an ambience that seems thinner the thicker it piles up; he manages to suggest, through non-stop juxtaposition, how arbitrary these indispensables are, so that when you come upon the Marcel Breuer coffee table, the gâteau St.-Honoré, the tensor lamp, the booklet of red tissue to prevent lipsticked lips from messing plush towels, these things seem not just whackily optional but, imaginatively, not worth having, and indeed there to stop you from imagining at all. In "Green Atom Number Five," the middle novella, two complacent monads guised as a fastidious couple find things vanishing from their exquisite new apartment: the Waring blender, paperweights, candelabra, even light bulbs, and they end up fighting each other naked in a *warehouse*. It's not just that the possessions eventually possess the possessors; it's much more complex, with possession becoming a figure against the dis-possession of space, with demonic possession going so far that (in its bourgeois materialist version at any rate, though the same may hold for taxidrivers and the poor with their monstrous sandwiches, 'custom-made' credenzas, and "stridently colored religious pictures") it becomes an epiphany concerning non-ownership: all one has is perceptions and there is no way of *owning them*. In other words, what other writers have done for silence, say, and blindness, Donoso does here for

José Donoso   (Photo: Layle Silbert)

intimate space; Roberto Ferrer the dentist and amateur painter keeps one room empty, with a naked bulb, a fatuous and dismal augury of what he and his wife discover at the end, after clawing blood from each other: his "obscene stomach over his whitish thin legs; she no different, her breasts withered, cellulite devouring her already flaccid hips," both of them just past forty, face to face "in an enormous emptiness of ground, immense angles, gigantic dimensions that might contain a door or a window or a single electric wire with a light fixture. The rest was space and more space in which the couple's puny howls were lost." A long last sentence dooms them to vacancy like two animals that will either pounce to destroy or possess or "flee, howling with fear, into the vast, empty space surrounding them." Not the least thing you could say about this story is that Pascal's fear of space's silence, William James's idea of vastation, and Lord Cherwell's question ("If space is curved, in what does it curve?")

come together to minify and ridicule the subject-object nexus that blots out *angst*.

More extremely, there is Sylvia Corday, the model, whose ears, mouth, and arms disappear from the gaze of a man whose sexual organs also go; and the prospect opens of the wholly dismantleable man, whom you fold up and carry about in a small suitcase. Not only do things not return our gaze; in gazing we reify—thingify—like the whistling adolescent who uses those around him as pretexts, props, and camouflage while matching their movements to private rhythms, such as those of 'Ondine.' "When he went for a walk, it was only to graze people's consciousness with a mere glance, with his whistling," which is, after all, only a more exalted version of the demotion applied to the sunburned nonagenarian whom, after a day in the park, the family bundles back into the car with "the six hundred other foldable objects." Indeed, at the end of "Gaspard de la Nuit," another youth takes over the whistler's 'life' while the whistler takes over his, and nobody notices the switch. The eye clones things *and* people, we conclude, even while it pretends to observe. Donoso's animated and interacting triptych is a beguiling excursion into the gruesomeness of automatic behavior and the seachanges inherent in perceivership. When he's done enough, certainly to earn him praise for patience and thoroughness, he does more, refining and integrating his concepts further; and, having done so, he does even more, pitching his tell at exquisite new registers of scrutiny. And, throughout, a Mrs. Presen feeds the protagonists' bodies while their minds dither helplessly on, a humdrum catalytic goddess out of the kitchen machinery.

Charleston and Other Stories is a more mixed performance, sometimes verging on the cuteness of a Just-So story, with the cogency minimally underpinned, but sometimes ampler (as when the fat man in the title story begins to dance as if evoking J. Scott Smart) or propulsively rich (as when a beast-haunted man who collects magazine photographs of tigers and jaguars and panthers finds his glossy bestiary coming ferally to life: a predictable but irresistibly stylish outcome). A dog-walking aunt, who mothers all but one of her nephews (he the narrator) by minutely adjusting their pillows and bedlinens, goes out one night and never comes back; the favored nephews age at speed while the narrator puts her to bed in his apple-pie story. In "The Güerro" a golden-haired WASP youth achieves an atavistic and fatal high at the source of a jungle river in a pastel fusion of Walter Pater and Joseph Conrad. Another story poignantly exposes the mind of a character born only to sleep. The blandness masks nothing and makes you keep your expectations down. And yet, although nothing in *Charleston and Other Stories* has the vertiginous abundance and multivalent wizardry of *Sacred Families*, this Donoso in a minor key is still an iridescent vertical invader of horizontal categories. The difference is that the surprises in *Charleston* are engaging and blithe; those in *Sacred Families* are irrevocable and, for all their sheen of ephemera gloatingly pinned onto cork, diagnostic of the human brain itself, done almost with a brain-side manner.

Coda to this creative *vendange*, the anecdotal, cosmopolitan archive called *The Boom* deals handily with the vogue for Latin American fiction, spraying the reader with names and titles, pointing out how foreign influences predominated over domestic ones, how the domestic hegemony was (and perhaps is) composed of staid and photographic simplists who were (and are) to the Latin American continent what the Eminent Victorians were to Imperial England, and debunking the gilded image of present-day Latin American novelists as jet-setting *bêtes de luxe*. Carlos Fuentes, flowering from *éminence grise* to *éminence rainbow*, gets full credit, as does the magazine *Mundo Nuevo*. It is a winningly readable account of a phenomenon that interests me less than some of the books that belong to it (and some that don't, such as the works of Onetti and Sábato, and that not exactly household title, *A Mute Girl's Notebook* by Margarita Aguirre). Donoso himself, as comprehensive as diffident, comes through vividly, standing on street corners to hawk *Veraneo* (1955), his first book of stories, swallowing an atrocious contract for *Coronation* (700 copies instead of an advance!), honoring Carpentier's *The Lost Steps* ("perching on the top . . . I was able for the first time to look beyond the barriers of simplicity and realism as our literature's sole destiny"), and Carlos Fuentes' *Where the Air is Clear* ("As I read it, literature took on another dimension"), and Cortázar's *Hopscotch*. What is clear is that the Boom was for long an underground yearning, fuelled by books "given, stolen, carried, recommended by friends" and never bought in a store or read because "urged by reviews or criticism." If only the useful index had been increased into a concise biographical/ bibliographical guide; we need to know more about the Boom authors least touted.

Most interesting of all, especially to those not eager to diagnose and tabulate the *Zeitgeist*, are the glimpses the book provides: of Vargas Llosa finishing *Conversation in The Cathedral* in a rat-infested London apartment; of Borges, at a Buenos Aires café table, asked if he knew Sanskrit ("Well, I don't know; just the Sanskrit that everyone knows"); of Donoso himself, writing in the garden of Carlos Fuentes' guest house while in the big house Carlos Fuentes writes *A Change of Skin* with Vivaldi's *Seasons* playing full blast. The Iowa workshop informs Donoso in 1965 that, instead of a course on the contemporary Spanish American novel, he might preferably do one on the poetry ("the novelists were unknown and of no interest to anyone"). Time moves slowly in Iowa, as on the Sun. Donoso confesses himself puzzled as to why "a novel as extraordinary and complex as *Herzog* could remain for so long on the bestseller lists," the answer maybe being that *Herzog* is ordinary and straightforward, which brings me to a question that Donoso skirts. Why the North American enthusiasm for austral work? My own quick answer would be that the Boom is the Great American Novel in drag, its stylishness and imaginative license tolerated because it emanates from within the penumbra of the rumba, whereas the GAN must be realistic. This is not the first time the United States has fawned on the exotic (had Dylan Thomas come from Des Moines, who

would have lapped him up?) while denouncing or ignoring comparable literary stylists in the home park at the same time as devoting inordinate space (any being inordinate) to the seafaring fustian of an actor called Sterling Hayden.

Truth told, and the Boom to the contrary, there are more reactionary editors and reviewers in positions of power than I recall from the Sixties, and I think we are in some danger of arguing: New York (as distinct from Germany, say) sponsored the Boom; Robert Coover reviews Donoso on the front page of the *Times Book Review* (as Ronald Christ gratefully points out in his introduction); ergo all is well. It is not. The North American literary sensibility thrives on contiguous exotophily, not on taste, respect for innovation, or distinguished style. The real test is what has happened to Carpentier and Lezama Lima up here, writers not too well-connected, one gathers, but of potent distinction. Nothing happened, happens. The pundits and tipsters and reputation-makers are happier with *One Hundred Years of Solitude*, which condition of comparative felicity makes one wonder if the land of Faulkner (the land that let him and Melville go out of print) heard a distant but similar-sounding drum and reviewed what it *thought* was there, glad to get away from the reservation (where puritanism reigns) and extol something childlike, non-science, non-mind, and, to the eye that sees what it wants to see, another Forsyte Saga done Mardi Gras fashion. José Donoso, whose work I continue to applaud (for reasons no doubt idiosyncratic), may well ponder the Darwin frog, found in a single forest of Chile and nowhere else, even though Earth has many similar forests. Should a Darwin frog grow north of the border, exotophiles would stiff it for dishonoring Mark Twain. ⬤

The Process Not the Poet

César Vallejo: The Dialectics of
Poetry and Silence
By Jean Franco
Cambridge University Press, 1976. $19.95

CANDACE SLATER

Because César Vallejo is a major twentieth-century poet, Jean Franco's *The Dialectics of Poetry and Silence*, the first study in any language to attempt a coherent overview of his writing, is both important and long overdue. Creating a backdrop against which the poet stands out as prototype for a new kind of artist, the book provides an understanding of the Peruvian writer, as well as the general evolution of twentieth-century poetry. Ultimately more interested in the nature of poetic discourse than in Vallejo or any one of his works, the book's essential drama is the formation of a new speaking voice. In good dialectic fashion, this focus on process rather than poet or individual poems accounts for many of its strengths as well as weaker points.

The Dialectics of Poetry and Silence represents a milestone in Vallejo scholarship. While the book looks to a sizeable body of previously existing criticism, none of this literature (including some excellent, in-depth studies from which the author clearly profits) offers a sustained vision of the writer's work. Part of the explanation for this lack of more comprehensive judgments lies in the relative inaccessibility of primary as well as secondary sources in the not-so-distant past. Though the last decade has

CANDACE SLATER, who teaches at Dartmouth College, has recently been awarded an NEH Summer Seminar Grant as well as a Tinker Grant to study contemporary Brazilian minstrels beginning this September.

witnessed a flurry of re-editions and translations, together with increasing quantities of critical discussion, much of the writer's work was previously unavailable and much, even today, remains in manuscript.[1] Added to these more-or-less logistical problems is the difficulty of Vallejo's verse. Given the complexity of his language, it is not surprising that recognition of his importance should be relatively slow. Although Vallejo's poems address many of the most fundamental problems of our century, the writer was so far before his time that only now, some four decades after his death in Paris, are we beginning to appreciate the impact, as well as object of his poems.

Vallejo's splintered, often hermetic expression is the inevitable touchstone for a study which seeks out the motives for peculiar phrases typified by "*el miércoles con uñas destronadas*" ("Wednesday with dethroned fingernails") that riddle (pun intended) virtually all of his verse. The book views Vallejo's literary career as an uneven progression from provincial poet vaguely dissatisfied with the inadequacies of the Christian Logos to thoroughly modern artist who co-opts the language of public oratory and sermon to challenge the very order this tradition represents. It therefore zeros in on the wrenched syntax and unconventional word play in individual poems as evidence of an ideological as well as esthetic "reorganization of hierarchies." The book does not attempt to solve the difficulties posed by Vallejo's language but sees these as response to larger questions encompassing literature and art.

Essentially chronological, the study poses a dialectical development in Vallejo's poetry by concentrating on the shifting position towards language represented by *Los heraldos negros*, 1919, *Trilce*, 1922 (English translation, 1974), *Poemas humanos*, 1939[2] (*Human Poems*, 1968) and *España, aparta de mí este cáliz*, 1937 (*Spain, Take This Cup From Me*, 1974). These books come to represent stages in a process marked by numerous antagonisms subsumed by the "poetry and silence" of the title. This titular "silence" refers to the implacable presence of the primary, physical world; "poetry" to often illusory realities associated with that secondary, because man-made apparatus, language."Species/individual, nature/culture are then the irreconcilable interests which thrust themselves into poetry itself," says the author, posing a tension between biological drives and social structures which reappears throughout the book. Seen in this light, the poems record an ongoing struggle between "the body as a living text" and "the clamor of words."

Such insistent focus on this evolution of a new poetic language has definite advantages. First, it allows a sophisticated, essentially linear consideration of Vallejo's artistic career that never degenerates into simply one more blow-by-blow account of a particular artist's life and oeuvre. Starting with an account of the all-important Christian Word as instrument of both domination and liberation in Vallejo's relatively isolated and impoverished highlands birthplace, the author is able to move into a compelling discussion of the disparity between "the insignificance of modern man" in Los heraldos negros and the Romantic exaltation of self versus post-Darwinian alienation in Trilce. The reader is thus well prepared for the counterpointing of "the solitude of print" and "the immediacy of the spoken word" in Human Poems, followed by the possibility of a new kind of man born of personal sacrifice in Spain, Take This Cup From Me, where the once-traditional bard suggests an all-encompassing human revolution.

This approach also provides a much-needed sense of cohesion in regarding this seemingly chaotic poet, a cohesion that does not deny but illumines his contradictions. These tensions are manifold and often provocative, because the opposition between "love" and "hate," "war" and "peace," "heat" and "cold" in scattered poems by Vallejo reflect larger thematic pulls such as Christian morality versus everyday reality, literacy versus illiteracy, and the rebellion against language versus a constant need for words. While these pairs are ultimately included in the nature/culture dialectic, they are interesting in their own right, and help to create a sense of dynamic

evolution highly appropriate to a poet whose entire life was marked by change. The author's spotlight on process avoids the pitfalls of either a formalism reluctant to consider the world in and of which the verse was created, or of a strictly sociological analysis that forces the outside world into each poem. The study sees Vallejo's writing as a series of acts involving a living subject rather than as a mere artifact inviting professional analysis.

Finally, the search that the book plots is in no way limited to Vallejo, but sheds light on a whole artistic generation. Because "consciousness and language are one" for this Peruvian writer "and there can no more be a new consciousness without a new language than there can be a new language without a new consciousness," his poetry cannot be separated from its historical context. In this larger arena, shifts in syntax signal profound changes in sensibility affecting not only the artist but society at large. "Metaphor based on analogy gives the illusory sense of coherence and makes the world into the poet's mirror or the poet into the mirror of the world," asserts the author. "Now the mirror is broken. Left with fragments of the old analogies, with dead metaphors and with a syntax which makes the 'I' the subject of willing and acting, the poet's task turns into an examination of the fragments or glimpses of the void." This statement is true not only for Vallejo, but encapsulates the essential drama of all contemporary art, be it modern poetry, electronic music, abstract painting or the stream-of-consciousness novel. The book makes clear that Vallejo is not looking for new poetic images or devices so much as a reality divorced from bankrupt political and economic institutions associated with a dead religion. Although well in the vanguard, he is by no means alone in the search for a new avenue of salvation that he himself describes as "the supremacy of the Word which discovers, which unites and which takes us beyond transient self interest and egoism." The author's marked skill in particularizing Vallejo's case without losing sight of the larger context is the book's major strength.

Naturally, this method also has its drawbacks. In this case, its bases are not sufficiently clear. Because all truly dialectical criticism evolves new categories from each work of art according to its unique inner logic, the reasons for these initial choices, and their definitions, must be absolutely plain. The book needs a fuller introductory discussion of such all-inclusive terms as "nature" and "culture," as well as more convincing reasons why these are so fundamental to Vallejo's thought. It also invites a fuller presentation of the genesis of this dialectic, which receives only cursory attention in the concluding paragraph. This brevity is disappointing because even readers thoroughly familiar with *The Presence of the Word* and *Grammatology* will not necessarily formulate the opposition represented by Walter Ong and Jacques Derrida in the same way as the author. If the book was meant to serve as the possible introduction to Vallejo suggested in the preface, the reader must participate as fully as possible in the evolutionary process. Because the language of the study, unlike the author's earlier *Modern Culture of Latin America*, draws heavily upon socio-linguistics, more detailed initial information would prepare even the uninitiated to appreciate the conflict posed and/or resolved by individual poems.

Furthermore, although the book does an admirable job of portraying the passage of the poetic voice from Orphic cry to the reflection of "ignorance and negation," its emphasis upon this diachronic sequence has certain curious side effects. Because, once again, the book's ultimate concern is less Vallejo than language, the reader finds it difficult on occasion to imagine not only the man but *a* man writing the poems. In its desire to compensate for previous "spiritual radiography" analyses that read into the verse a distorting martyr-prophet-hero, the study maintains a distance from the individual and his immediate environment that makes him somewhat abstract. The consciousness so far outshadows the personality in some moments that the reader tends to cling to concrete details that he would otherwise forget: one of Vallejo's

grandmothers was named Natividad Gurrionero, the poet had two girlfriends named Maria, he refused to cut his long hair. It would be possible to strengthen the reader's sense of both Vallejo and his particular place in history without resorting to anecdote by following up on various comparisons with Pablo Neruda that are introduced but never developed and by creating a clearer sense of the Peruvian writer's relationships with other contemporaries who, although mentioned, remain primarily names.

Finally, the overview that distinguishes the book from others on Vallejo is almost too successful on occasion, making the poems seem programmed, the poet a monomaniac. The holistic character of the study is less fruitful in those moments when the author strains each detail to support and reflect the totality. Therefore, while most readers will find the majority of textual analyses cogent, some will regard certain readings as either one-sided or forced. All will not be convinced, for instance, that the mother who *"como una Dolorosa, entra y sale"* ("who, like a Dolorosa, comes and goes") in the poem "Encaje de fiebre" ("Feverlace") necessarily signifies "the synchronic pattern of human relationships" or that the kite strings over which the children quarrel in *Trilce* 52 are meant along with smoke and the letters of the alphabet to suggest "individual destinies" in contrast to the air, dung and trees. The author insists that "Vallejo's poetic language is marked by intention," but given the relative dearth of writing by the poet on his own work, it is difficult to know precisely how far this intentionality extends. Thus, while it is fair to assume that Vallejo deliberately cloaked his rebellion in hermetic language because "his devastating attack on the individualized subject was too radical to permit him to dispense with parody, irony and word play," this type of assertion is difficult or impossible to prove. Some readers will not be troubled by the lack of proof, arguing that it makes little difference how or why a pattern emerges, if the author can show that it exists. Others will be less comfortable with the study's repeated insistence on Vallejo's extraordinary level of consciousness, questioning not the author's logic, but her degree of certitude.

In short then, the book's stress on process has advantages as well as some drawbacks. Jean Franco is particularly good at drawing upon many different sources to create a panoramic vision whose breadth does not preclude a sense of order over time. Although far more remains to be written on the multiple aspects of Vallejo's writing (his prose and drama, for instance, could only be touched on in this study), *The Dialectics of Poetry and Silence* represents an invaluable starting point. In its attempts at demystification, sensitivity to oppositions, concern for social context and, above all, obvious fascination with the multiple problems of language, the study bears a limited but nevertheless real resemblance to Val-lejo's poetry. Striving throughout to show how the Peruvian writer's verse arises from a lifelong struggle *"entre el decirlo y el callarlo"* or "poetry and silence," the author shows how words become the means to a new, all-important Word.

[1] In an introduction to a bilingual edition of *Poemas Humanos: Human Poems* (New York: Grove Press, 1968), Clayton Eshleman asserts that as many as four full-length plays, two novels, two collections of essays, a film script, a half-dozen notebooks and a volume of miscellaneous prose remain unpublished.

[2] *Poemas humanos* was published posthumously by the poet's widow. Because the poems were written and revised over a considerable period of time, both their order and some versions have aroused controversy.

Political Religion

The Gospel of Solentiname
By Ernesto Cardenal
Translated by Donald D. Walsh
Orbis, 1976. $6.95

In Cuba
By Ernesto Cardenal
Translated by Donald D. Walsh
New Directions, 1974.
$10.50 (hardcover); $3.95 (paper)

RAYMOND A. SCHROTH

Christianity is—if not in its transcendent origins, then certainly in its human incarnation—by history and necessity a political religion. Its mysteries cannot, of course, find adequate expression in one political party; but once God is understood as revealing himself uniquely, "pouring himself out," in one particular man—in one concrete political and social context—the political implications of all Jesus said and did inevitably make demands on us today.

For, although he refused political power (indeed fled from it as from Satan's snare) there was nothing apolitical about Jesus. He knew that his teaching threatened the interlocking political and religious power structures, and the Jewish high priests and Romans who did him in correctly perceived that Jerusalem—and, in a larger sense, the world—was not big enough for both the vision of universal brotherhood preached to the poor and the cynicism and imperialism of Caiaphas and Caesar.

Unfortunately, since the death of Jesus, a good percentage of those who call themselves Christian have learned to live comfortably with cynicism and Caesar. In spite of its doctrinal dedication to social justice, reaffirmed in the social encyclicals of Popes Leo XIII, Pius XI, John XXIII and even in the ambivalent leadership of Paul VI, the Roman Catholic church is seldom perceived as committed to the oppressed. Except for the sporadic reappearances of the worker-priest movement in France. And except for Latin America where the so-called Libera-

RAYMOND A. SCHROTH, S.J., is associate editor of *Commonweal* and associate professor at Fordham University where he celebrates his liturgy almost nightly with students.

tion Theology—based on a Marxist reading of the Scriptures—has inspired, on the one hand, hope in those yearning for an interpretation of their faith that integrates their thirst for God and their hunger for justice and, on the other hand, has raised questions for traditional theologians who insist that to link God's word to a strictly political cause is to risk compromising the power of the word and to promise to the oppressed something that true religion was never intended to deliver.

Ernesto Cardenal is not a theologian. He is that odd but rich combination: Nicaraguan poet, priest, Marxist, revolutionary. Born in Granada, Nicaragua in 1925, in 1957 he entered the Trappist monastery in Gethsemane, Kentucky, where Thomas Merton was his spiritual director. He left because of poor health in two years, and for a while joined the Benedictines at Cuernavaca, Mexico; but, moved more toward active pastoral work, he was ordained in 1965 and founded a Christian commune, with a clinic and artists center, among poor fishermen and farmers on the island of Solentiname in Lake Nicaragua. There his reputation as a poet has grown, and there each Sunday the townspeople gather around for his dialogue liturgies where God's word once again brings hope to the poor and makes the authorities nervous.

In Cuba is a journal and an anthology of other Latin American poets compiled during Cardenal's two visits to Cuba: one for several months in 1970, as a guest of Casa de las Américas to sit on a poetry panel; the other a quick trip to spend several hours whirling around Havana talking religion with Fidel Castro, whose theology is barely distinguishable from Cardenal's. His record of the visit is by no means a systematic, critical study of the status of the Revolution. Rather it resembles, as much as anything, Edward Bellamy's 1888 utopian novel, Looking Backward, where the hero awakens in 2000 A.D. Boston and is given a guided tour of the future egalitarian, regimented society where either freedom has taken on a new definition or the populace is too content to realize it is not free. Cardenal's brief chapters are, for the most part, accounts of

his visits to various institutions—like the People's Courts, a psychiatric hospital, or a Country Club turned National Art School—that have been reformed by the Revolution, plus encounters with citizens, students, church and government officials, and celebrities (like Camilo Torres' mother) who testify to the Revolution's effect on their lives. "One place where the tenderness of the Revolution may be seen is in the Psychiatric Hospital of Havana. The insane are in pavilions with floors as shiny as those of a luxury hotel."

Strictly speaking, although the book's form resembles a traveling intellectual's journal, Cardenal's observations are surprisingly unreflective, and he manifests little of the healthy scepticism and critical intelligence anyone might expect from a journalist or an intellectual. I do not quarrel with his evidence that Castro's Cuba is an infinitely more just society than Batista's, or with his lament that Cuban Catholicism remains reactionary, unpersecuted and unpurified, or with his conclusion that the true practice of religion—sacrifice and brotherly love—can thrive more effectively in a Marxist than in a capitalist society. But I do grow impatient with any form of dogmatism, or any too-readily-invoked value system that smacks of idolatry, whether it be Holy Mother Church, the Revolution, the States, the Presidency, Big Brother or el Ché.

The function of the Christian gospel, it seems to me, with its doctrine of the cross, is to make this kind of political idolatry impossible, to pass judgment on any aspect of any political system that diminishes human dignity and freedom, not to bless or consolidate the power of any political bloc, no matter how benevolent it may be. Thus the priest-activist Daniel Berrigan, S.J., has said that even if George McGovern had been elected president he himself would still belong outside the White House gates ready to raise protest.

Cardenal, of course, is a poet and mystic, not an intellectual; but he is a priest, a public man, a custodian of the gospel in a special way. So I have mixed feelings in The Gospel of Solentiname (otherwise a beautiful little book, both physically and spiritually), a collection of his community dia-logues, when the parishioners supposedly meditating aloud at the Eucharist fall again and again into revolutionary slogans. No matter what the gospel, the discussion is inevitably political, someone always leads the prayer around to the class struggle: "And the holy or jubilee year now means that people go to Rome and pray in the churches and receive a papal blessing. But the holy year should be agrarian reform and the socialization of all means of produc-tion." Considering Herod's slaughter of the Innocents, one speaker says: "But I say, the child is not always going to be tiny. I say to my brothers, my comrades: Hell, they're

screwing us! We're giving them everything we have! Let's fight! That's what Christ did." That, precisely, is *not* what Christ did and Cardenal should know that. When Jesus predicts persecution, another in the group says: "At the same time he's telling us that we must be aggressive and peaceful. I understand it this way: When you have to use violence, use it, and when you can do things peacefully, do them peacefully. It's only a matter of tactics, I say."

Well, I say, it's not only a matter of tac-tics; and I wish Father Cardenal had ex-plained that before going on with the Eu-charistic prayer. ◯

The Self-Made Poet

Alfonsina Storni, From Poetess to Poet
By Rachel Phillips
Tamesis, 1975. $12.50

JUDITH A. WEISS

If there is one major dilemma facing female academics, it is the resolution of their am-biguous role as females molded, and func-tioning, in a male academic tradition. The concept of the "female eunuch" is being replaced by a far more positive self-image which recognizes—and accepts—the two streams that make a female academic and can safely be termed the androgynous be-ing. This view is gaining sufficient accept-ance so that a study like this one by Rachel Phillips does not appear as a radical threat to scholarship. It represents, rather, a move-ment out of the predominantly male modes

JUDITH A. WEISS teaches Latin American lit-erature at Mount Allison University. Her book on the *Casa de las Américas* will appear this summer.

of perception in judging women writers, towards the integration of rigorous scholar-ship with a responsible and progressive stand on questions of female identity.

Equally important, beyond the needs of the individual scholars, are the needs of the students of Hispanic literature (a very high percentage of whom are women). These stu-dents are exposed to a cursory, standard curriculum of women writers, usually grouped together as "the women writers" (especially the poets), and interpreted by male critics and by teachers, male and fe-male, molded in a patriarchal profession. Books like this one are the beginning of a constructive alternative.

Ms. Phillips proposes to trace the evolu-tion of Alfonsina Storni as a self-made poet who transcended/evolved beyond the styles, themes and poetic personality that had been the hallmark of the *poetess*—a sorry term that can be equated with the idea of a sub-standard, sex-limited poet.

Female poets in Latin America can be seen, both synchronically and diachronic-ally, as sad cases of underdevelopment within a wider underdevelopment. Storni's achievement was to break out of that posi-tion by exploiting the objective factors available to her (the influences in her early, uninformed days, and, later, literary circles into which she quietly forced her presence), and by altering her own subjective elements (self-image, lyrical voice). Rachel Phillips' achievement has been to bring the evolution of this remarkable literary figure into proper focus.

She studies Storni's poetry collections in individual chapters, under the headings of: Poetry of Apprenticeship (La inquietud del Rosal), Poems of Love (El dulce daño, Irremediablemente and Languidez), Poetry of Self-Knowledge (Ocre), Poetry of Things Seen (Mundo de Siete Pozos), and Poetry in the Shadow of Death (Mascarilla y trébol). There is, in addition, a separate chapter on Storni's dramatic works, including her children's theater (which ranks among the most sensitive and accomplished in the field). An appendix summarizes Storni's most significant prose publications.

Ms. Phillips' approach is thorough and eclectic: she weaves Storni's intellectual and personal biography with textual analyses, never losing the main thread of the study (the idea of Storni's poetic evolution). There is substantial unity of purpose in the whole, and the author develops convincing arguments by drawing quite skillfully on the existing criticism and studies on Storni and on more contemporary views and theory. There is for her a viable connection between detail and generality, and she makes good use of this interaction in exploring Storni's development as a writer.

One of the problems in redefining the work of a female poet involves the idea of femaleness, and how the poet herself views it. A view that was until quite recently prevalent among critics hinged on the equation of 'female' with 'feminine': the female is thereby primarily essence, and, aside from that, limited to a capability for extreme loving and hating, determined usually by her emotional and irrational impulses (feminine behaviour). The female/feminine idea could manifest itself in poetic creations that were supposedly hampered by women's inability to transcend; it was consequently expressed in writing that tended to be imitative and explored few themes beyond the realm of passion or subjectivity. Such poetic modes were applauded by (male) critics in a benign, patronizing manner, as quaint and charming

in a decorative or secondary sort of way.

This kindliness often reached its limits whenever a female author asserted her literary personality beyond the respectable boundaries set for her sex. She might, of course, gain acceptance by rejecting or playing down elements of her writing that could be identified as "female" or "feminine." Either way, she was negating her total sexuality or placing constraints on it. The breakthrough, as Phillips accurately points out in Storni's case, can occur when the writer stops automatically identifying "female" with "feminine." In the case of most developed women writers, one can usually observe a reappraisal of their gender identity and an evolution away from traditional "feminine" modes (viz., roles) while coming to terms with the primal self in all its femaleness.

The kind of repressive tolerance practiced, apparently, by a majority of traditional critics with regard to women writers is something with which Phillips clearly has little patience, although she presents quite fairly both favorable and unfavorable criticism of Storni's work. We are reminded that erotic poetry was acceptable—within limits: the baring of emotions and of an active sexuality was profoundly distasteful to a number of Storni's contemporaries, like José Fernández Coria, who recommended that she no longer continue to write poetry: "En vez de escribir versos, procure inspirarlos. Es más femenino." ("Instead of writing verse, try to inspire it. It's more feminine.") It is interesting, however, that, in reacting to her excessively "effusive erotic lyricism," Fernández Coria also alluded to what could be an objective weakness in Storni's poetry. He was obviously too caught up in his moral indignation to phrase his criticism in a level-headed manner, and Phillips, in turn, reacts strictly to his sexist moralizing. Yet throughout her study she does make literary judgments that praise Storni's emergence from the erotic mold and from her earlier dependence on pathetic fallacy and loose imagery. Contemporaries of Storni ended up lamenting her "loss of lyricism" which, for Rachel Phillips, amounts to an emergence from the anachronistic, underdeveloped stages of development.

The difference between the two critics lies in recognizing the validity of the female identity in its erotic or sexual expressions, which Phillips does, while restricting her criticism to Storni's writing. Accordingly, she praises, as Storni's more responsible contemporaries did, the maturing process of the poet: the tightened imagery (through increased use of metaphor), the development of objectivity, the more self-confident voice.

There is in this study a conservative appraisal of Storni's absolute bitterness toward men. Phillips seems quite skeptical of the extreme pessimism Storni expressed, particularly in her plays, about the prospects for improving relations between the sexes. The problem with some of Storni's passionate writing is, admittedly, the weakening of its literary merit for the benefit of the message; Phillips' view, which might be open to ideological criticism, is that it is the extreme nature of the message that makes the plays, for instance, unconvincing.

But Phillips opts, whenever she can, for a sensible compromise—and I use the term "sensible" as an alternative to, or interchangeable with, "objective," since this book, tacitly recognizing the very real limits of objectivity, strives for an informed, balanced appraisal, and its conclusions are based largely on a common-sense approach to the problems. This is partly what enables her to criticize simultaneously Storni's anti-male bias and her lapses into traditional "feminine" modes. She is also fair in her exploration of Storni's self-destructive impulse, which one might see as connected to a passive sort of fatalism, a succumbing to the "essential" determinants of one's life. Phillips is careful to trace Storni's suicidal tendencies to the years *before* she became ill with cancer; she also attempts to analyze these tendencies as a consequence of her early family life with a psychologically absent, and rejecting, father. Horacio Quiroga's influence on Storni, as a close friend, is also mentioned in this context. (Quiroga's life, of course, can be read as a series of tragic deaths of close relatives and friends, climaxing in his own suicide.) Both Quiroga and Storni's father appear in "Ultrat(e)léfono," a

dramatic sonnet recounting a telephone conversation with the two dead men.

All through the study, the figure presented to us is ambivalent. Storni's poetic development involved at least two parallel dynamics. On the one hand, her themes ranged, over the years, from the most personal to the most universal, from the erotic to the existential; at the same time her language, her voices, and her symbols evolved from her early poetry (where, as a shy and modest school teacher, she looked tentatively to the more traditional and "safe" influences at a time when Huidobro was taking his bold, light-year leaps) to her last volumes, where a confident poet was making those intelligent choices that distinguish influence from dependence. Storni had the ability to choose the influences that would encourage, rather than stunt, the growth of her artistic personality.

On the other hand, she never rejected her female consciousness, but tended rather to embrace it and explore its full potential. As a result she rarely rejected the world of emotion, but attempted to invert the terms of reference that had traditionally limited the female poet (poetess) to the ghetto of indiscriminate emotionalism.

It is quite true that Storni may have (mainly in her dramatic works) shouted her anger and frustration above the respectable decibel-levels of balanced poetics. But, at the same time, her finest poetry includes some of the most devastating lines since Sor Juana Inés de la Cruz against misogyny and male-imposed limitations. One of Storni's most effective devices was to hold up a mirror to the male, thereby acknowledging herself as Other, but as conscious and active Other, engaged in her own liberation, hence superior to her oppressor, himself a slave of his role:

You want me white;
You want me like surf,
Like mother-of-pearl.
To be a lily,
Above all lilies, chaste.
With a subtle perfume.
A shut corolla.

Not filtered by a single
Ray of moonlight.
With no daisy
To call herself my sister.
You want me like snow;
You want me white;
You want me chaste.

You, who had
All goblets handy,
Lips purple
With fruit and honey.
You who at the banquet,
Covered with grape leaves,
Left your flesh
Celebrating Bacchus.
You, who dressed in red
Ran havoc
In the dark
Gardens of Deceit.
You, who keep
Your skeleton intact
I know not
By what miracles
(God have mercy on you),
You expect me to be chaste
(God have mercy on you),
You expect me to be pure.

Flee to the woods;
Go to the mountain;
Wash out your mouth;
Live in cabins;
Touch the moist earth
With your hands;
Feed your body
With bitter roots;
Drink from the rocks;
Sleep on the frost;
Renew your tissues
With saltpeter and water;

Speak with the birds
And get up at dawn.
And when your flesh
Returns to normal,
And when you've put
Your soul in it,
Which had become snarled
In bedrooms,
Then, my good man,

Expect me to be white,
Like snow,
Expect me to be chaste.

Storni was impatient with the Male, but one might be somewhat more indulgent than Phillips toward a woman, alone from the age of sixteen, in a world dominated by males and by deceit. That, however, is the tender ideological issue.

Phillips is careful not to overestimate Storni's stature, and concludes that Storni was in fact a minor poet, both in terms of her time and, from a diachronic perspective, as a female poet (when compared, for instance, with Sappho or other major women writers). By stating this, she can offer a twofold justification of her study: her interest in minor poets, because they often reflect their world more completely than major figures, and her rejection of the sexist "myth" that a woman poet deserves special attention because she is female (inflating a writer's achievement by virtue of non-literary criteria is indulging in chivalrous insults).

The final conclusion of this study is that Storni is "able to survive a demotion—or rather a promotion—from the upper ranks of women poets, into the place which is properly hers as a maker, a poet in the true sense of the word." The terms "demotion" and "promotion" might be interpreted by some as an implicit downgrading of the value of studying women writers qua women. I am not in any way defending mediocrity, and I would advocate, as Phillips does, a sensible evaluation of female as well as male writers. There is, however, in exclusively non-gender ranking, the potential danger that whenever standard curricula are compiled only the top-ranking poets would be included, and minor poets like Storni would be ignored. At present—whether for chivalrous or for feminist considerations—students (and, one might add, potential writers) are exposed to some of their more valuable writings. It is a two-edged sword, and the debate about ranking writers will no doubt go on indefinitely. Perhaps the most sensible solution does lie in women's studies curricula that, as adjuncts to standard courses on Poetry, Art, etc., would ensure that the good though secondary female poets are studied objectively.

Objections will be raised that this question is not relevant to literature. They can be countered by a reminder that female writers, like female critics, have been involved traditionally in a personal struggle with strong political overtones. It is usually by coming to grips with the contradictions inherent in being a female and a poet/ scholar that women have evolved from, or transcended, their underdevelopment. And a realization of this is what might well encourage the production of further critical studies of the quality of this one. ⬤

An Oral Collage

The Fair
By Juan José Arreola
Translated by John Upton
University of Texas Press, 1977. $10.95.

EDITH GROSSMAN

The Fair, by Juan José Arreola, translated by John Upton, is the ironic portrait of the fictitious Mexican town of Zapotlán. It is an oral portrait rendered as a collage composed of many voices—townspeople past and present—juxtaposed in a seemingly disjointed fashion and heard over and over again throughout the novel. The voices speak at random with no regard for chronology, as if the narrative were the stream-of-consciousness of the town itself. A shoemaker struggles to survive his first attempt at farming, a child makes his weekly confession, landowners seethe because the Indians are suing for restoration of lands stolen from them over the centuries, a lovelorn adolescent

EDITH GROSSMAN, the author of *The Anti-Poetry of Nicanor Parra,* is currently translating the poetry of Macedonio Fernández.

keeps his romantic diary, the provincial literary society earnestly pursues high culture —slowly, by means of accumulated detail, contrapuntal versions of the same event, and proliferating points of view, the life and people of Zapotlán take on form, substance and significance. The reader is only momentarily confused by the welter of voices, themes and sub-plots. These soon become familiar and recognizable even though they are out of sequence, for language and the structure of the novel itself are not the object of experimentation in this book. Syntax and vocabulary undergo no Joycean twistings or re-creations; *The Fair* is much more a sardonic and basically realistic document of small town hypocrisy, frustration and meanness than a technical or stylistic tour-de-force.

The event which gives the book its title is the annual Fair held in honor of St. Joseph, patron saint of Zapotlán. This year the religious celebration begins and ends with a typical, defining violence that seems to symbolize the sanctimonious dishonesty and brutality of the landed classes. These respectable folk think the Indian Communities should contribute generously to the costs of the Fair and be content in return to carry the heavy floats in the religious processions. They are willing, however, to go to criminal lengths to stop the Indians' pursuit of legal redress. Landowners force field hands at gun point to bear false witness against the leaders of the Indian effort. The priest, victim of innuendo, is replaced by a younger man whose sympathies lie in more appropriate directions. In the brutal racial struggle for control of the land, venality and contempt drive men to acts of malice, fraud and violence. They take a savage pleasure in the disrupted lives of their neighbors, and at the same time they revel in the meretricious odor of sanctity that surrounds the "unwavering Catholicism" of Zapotlán and its citizens.

The Fair, like the lawsuit of the Indians, functions as a major unifying theme in the novel. Both bring out the worst in the townspeople of Zapotlán, whose greed and talent for deception are heightened by their vehement response to the litigation and by the unexpected Pontifical Coronation of St. Joseph as the town's patron saint. These seemingly disparate and unrelated motifs converge significantly at several points in the novel, when each appears to be an ironic commentary on the other. A prime example is the case of Señor Farías, a wealthy businessman who arranges for the coronation of the saint and, in the name of Zapotlán and with the old priest's promise of payment, purchases four kilos of gold to be used for crowns for the images of the Holy Family. As his support for the Indian cause is made public, the higher clergy, the banking interests and the state authorities combine to cut off his credit and not reimburse him for the money spent on the crowns. He is a radical danger to the local vested interests for, as we are told by one of the most insidious of the voices, the high salaries he pays his workers could "upset the economy of the entire region."

Despite the tensions and cross currents generated by several different conflicts of interest, this community portrait holds no real surprises or revelations for the reader. Life in the provinces is exactly what we have learned to expect: tedious, hypocritical, oppressive, conventional—this is a small town in the grim mode of Sinclair Lewis and Sherwood Anderson. Nothing magical or mysterious or marvelous helps to justify or explain the nastiness in Zapotlán, a place far removed from either Macondo or Our Town. There is, unfortunately, a predictability in the action, the character types, the ambience, the unspoken indignation of the author that recalls the thesis novels of an earlier and perhaps less morally ambivalent time. We have all been there before, and no matter how much of a social reality may be reflected in these conventions they are still literary cliches, and the book suffers artistically because of them. They intrude on the finely etched observation which is a major novelistic achievement in *The Fair*.

The translation captures the nuances of character expressed by each of the voices. Mr. Upton is extremely sensitive to language and handles the difficult changes of diction with great skill. Whether the tone is colloquial or formal, the translator consistently maintains decisive control of the material. The woodcuts by Barbara Whitehead are expressive in their own right and add an important and pleasurable dimension to the experience of reading the book.

Untangling Aztec Literature

Introduction to Classical Nahuatl
By J. Richard Andrews
University of Texas Press, 1975.
Text $39.50; Workbook $14.95; Set $52.50

JOHN BIERHORST

It is undoubtedly true, as the literary anthropologist D. G. Brinton observed nearly a hundred years ago, that Classical Nahuatl, or Aztec, offers "special recommendations" to anyone "who would acquaint himself with an American language." Not the least of these "recommendations" is the existence of a surprisingly large corpus of poetry, prayer, oratory, history, myth, reportage, and even theater, recorded by native scribes who had learned to write their own language in the new Latin script and who were willing to preserve what they could of their heritage during the chaotic decades immediately following the Conquest. Today the Aztec manuscripts surviving from this period hold more promise for the literary investigator than any other body of American Indian literature.

But by Brinton's time Classical Nahuatl had long since fallen into disuse, and the expertise of sixteenth-century linguist-missionaries was likewise a thing of the past. In 1885 Rémi Siméon had effectively launched modern Aztec studies with his admirable *Dictionnaire de la Langue Nahuatl*, yet progress from then on was not rapid.

JOHN BIERHORST, whose books include *The Red Swan* and *Four Masterworks of American Indian Literature*, is at work on a new translation of *Cantares Mexicanos*.

Only with much diffidence did Brinton publish his *Ancient Nahuatl Poetry* in 1890; and these translations, while still admired for their loveliness, do in fact contain so many errors as to render them all but worthless. Much better work was done by the German ethnologist Eduard Seler during the period 1900-1920, though Seler limited his efforts almost exclusively to myth and reportage.

About 1940 the first and only concentrated attack on the mysteries of Nahuatl poetry, rhetoric, and drama was launched in Mexico itself by the Franciscan Angel M. Garibay. The translations published by this distinguished investigator have aroused much sympathetic curiosity, and a few choice excerpts have even been widely quoted. But it should be clear that Garibay's work is only tentative. Indeed, the suspicion voiced by J. Richard Andrews in the book I am about to discuss, that Garibay's translations are at times "closer to invention," is not unjustified.

Throughout the fundamental problem has been the lack of a comprehensive modern grammar—and it is this lack that Andrews has remedied, in one brilliant stroke, with his *Introduction to Classical Nahuatl*. It is no exaggeration to say that this book is the most significant contribution to Aztec language study since Siméon's dictionary (in fact, Andrews' depth of comprehension far exceeds Siméon's). Moreover, it is one of those rare, elegant works that serve the beginner as well as the expert. With this volume in hand, specialists will be able to correct their errors, and amateurs who wish to learn the language will be able to do so without fear of disappointment.

Though indebted to the seventeenth-century grammar of Horacio Carochi and, to a lesser extent, grammars written even earlier, Andrews' presentation of the language is spectacularly original, derived at least in part from his own analysis of native texts and old vocabularies. Carrying the unmistakable imprint of structuralist thought, it is a work that could only have been produced in our time. Conversely, it is free of philosophical burdens, free of jargon. And what really matters is that the method works.

The 500-page textbook, which doubles as a reference grammar, includes forty-eight progressive "lessons." The workbook, designed for self-teaching, provides an "exercise" (with answers) for each of the "lessons." It is a deliberately old-fashioned, uncompromising kind of workbook, reminiscent of Latin verb-and-noun drills. Though not exhaustive, the course is rigorous, and the reader who completes it will be able to proceed directly to the ancient texts:

*In ye nelli ayāxcān in cocōc īhua, tlaōcōltica
    tinemih ihua.*
(Though in truth the misery be scarcely drunk,
    life is a painful drink.)

A word-for-word, lexical translation of the same line will give an idea of the underlying structure of the language:

The already it-is-a-truth scarcely the
    it-is-a-misery it-is-drunk, it-is-pain-wise
    we-are-living it-is-drunk.

Notice how many of the words are complete sentences in themselves. The principal virtue of Andrews' method is that it enables the student to deal successfully with this curious feature. But rather than try to describe the method in detail, I would prefer to give some account of what we may now expect when it comes to deciphering the literature.

Of all the Aztec documents worthy of investigation, two will continue to be of primary interest. These are (1) the famous Florentine Codex, an enormous twelve-tome repository of things Aztec, and (2) the codex *Cantares Mexicanos*, the richest source of Aztec verse and drama.

The following brief quotation from Book Six, Chapter Eighteen, of the Florentine Codex (unquestionably the more accessible of the two manuscripts) will perhaps convey something of the highly organized nature of Aztec verbal art—a characteristic that has heretofore been obscured. In this passage a nobleman is addressing his daughter on the occasion of her coming of age. The translation, my own, has been made according to Andrews' precepts:

It is a good time now and a good time yet, for your heart is yet jade, yet turquoise. Still it is waking, still nothing spoils it. It is still sprouting; it is yet unbranched. It is still whole, still pure, still undefiled.

Observe that every image, bar none, contributes to the metaphorical picture of the unopened (green) bud. But the metaphor does not emerge in any previous translation; it has been hidden for four hundred years. If Aztec literature has seemed a bit chaotic—charming, perhaps, but unformed—it is only because its inner threads have been consistently tangled by imprecise readings; and although Andrews does not teach this point, the student who now works carefully with the Florentine Codex, especially Book Six, should soon discover it for himself.

The *Cantares Mexicanos* will prove more difficult. The three scholars who have approached it thus far (Brinton, Garibay, and Leonhard Schultze Jena) have had only limited success. Nor has anyone even managed to get all the way through it. The poetry bristles with puns, nonce words, and euphonic vocables. Nonetheless, it would seem that this fascinating codex is now ready to yield.

Of the several tiny extracts that have become well-known through the efforts of Garibay and his school, the following may serve as a typical specimen. Garibay's own reading, which devotees of pre-Columbian poetry will recognize immediately, is roughly this:

My friends, please hear:
it is the song of a dream:
each spring the golden (maize) ear
gives us life:
the ruddy ear gives us a cool drink:
it adorns us with a necklace of precious stones
to know that the hearts of our friends
are true to us.

It appears, however, that a more accurate reading would be something like this:

O friends, hear a song of the Dream:
as the gold ear of summer sustains us,
as the rubiate ear gives us life,
it bejewels us to know that friends' hearts go forth to do the Real planting.

A king is here addressing his soldiers, whom he is about to include in one of those peculiar religious wars, the purpose of which was to obtain captives for sacrifice. Later, the victims' hearts, still beating, will be wrenched from their opened breasts and ritually fed to the sun or the earth, thus insuring the growth of crops. The hearts, then, do the "real" planting, "real" in the double sense of "actual" and "sacred." Notice the antithesis between the "Dream," which is human life, and that which is "Real," implying the hereafter. We know, in fact, that sacrificial victims were promised eternal life. And the larger poem, from which these lines have been extracted, takes this promise as its central theme. In essence, the king is telling his warriors: "Go and die that I may live; in dying, ye shall live!" The ambiguity is typically Aztec.

Garibay, though partially correct in his interpretation of these lines, makes three grammatical errors that prevent full comprehension. He reads *ithuitia* ("to impart vision;" figuratively, "to impart life") as though it were *itia* ("to give a drink"). He ignores the purposive verb-ending *to* ("to go in order to do"), which in the *Cantares Mexicanos* carries the idiomatic connotation, "to go forth from this life," and he mistranslates *tlaneltoca* as "be true to us." *Tlaneltoca* ("to keep the faith") is a pun, moreover, on *tlaneltōca* (literally, "to plant things in a real manner"), which I here give as "do the Real planting." This is not to imply, however, that Garibay's work is valueless. On the contrary, it abounds in helpful hints and will continue to serve scholars for years to come. All I am saying is that we are now ready to go farther.

Though much work remains to be done before Aztec literature can be classified as known—especially in its larger forms—it seems reasonably clear that the way is open. As new talent is recruited, progress will surely be made. It is to be hoped that the singular brilliance of Andrews' work will succeed in attracting a higher level of contribution than the subject has heretofore been able to command.

Still Discovering the New World

Pre-Columbian Art of South America
By Alan Lapiner
Harry N. Abrams, Inc., 1976. $50.00

DIANA FANE

There is a new self-consciousness about approaches to the ancient arts of the Americas. Occasioned by the bicentennial, several
publications have traced European attitudes
toward art and civilization in the New
World from the time of the first contacts to
the present. The result is a fascinating chapter in the history of ideas, and a sobering
reminder of the influence of our expectations on our perceptions. The story is by no
means over, however. Not only have attitudes changed, allowing us to accept as art
what was previously regarded as barbarian
relic, but the evidence itself has changed,
making it necessary to continually revise our
conception of the scope and content of pre-
Columbian artistic traditions. The kind of
art that delighted Albrecht Dürer at the time
of the conquest—precious objects of gold
and delicate featherwork—was almost all
destroyed in the 16th century along with
the major religious statues. The masterpieces of a century were, therefore, lost forever. On the other hand, the existence of
remarkable works of art from earlier epochs
was not revealed until much later. Abandoned Maya cities escaped notice until the
middle of the 19th century, and Machu Pic-
chu, one of the most dramatic Inca sites, remained unknown until 1911. The New
World was not discovered all at once.

South America, in particular, has revealed
its esthetic heritage slowly. Nineteenth-cen-
tury travelers to this area delighted in the

DIANA FANE, who is writing a study of Aztec
sculpture, works in the Egyptian department of
the Metropolitan Museum of Art.

exotic flora and fauna of the tropical forests
and rhapsodized over the juxtaposition of
sea, desert, and mountain in Peru, but said
little about past art since little was visible.
Monumental sculpture in stone was con-
spicuous by its absence. Nature has dominated art in descriptions of South America
because nature, in that part of the world, is
so obvious. The grandeur and diversity of
the landscape are impossible to ignore; the
art works from which our knowledge of
South American cultural tradition derives
are the opposite—small in scale, cryptic in
their symbolism, and hidden from view.
Peru is a land of buried treasures. What is
more, the privacy of the tomb is often vio-
lated only to be replaced by that of the
private collection thanks to the tireless activity of grave looters. As a result much of
Peruvian art remains hidden.

In a field where so much material is inaccessible, there is a real need for a pictorial
survey that considers all the evidence. Alan
Lapiner's beautiful book illustrating over
900 examples of South American art ranging
in date from 1400 B.C. to A.D. 1532 is,
therefore, especially welcome. As the majority of the pieces are here published for
the first time, anyone opening the book will
experience a sense of discovery.

Architecture and stone sculpture are not
included. Lapiner has concentrated on those
objects whose specialness is not only evi-
denced by technical excellence and icono-
graphic complexity, but is attested to by the
fact that they served as burial offerings,
carefully selected and perhaps even speci-
fically made to accompany an important individual in his grave. Although coming from
many different areas and periods in time,
these objects have in common their small
scale, rich symbolism, and final participation in a cult of the dead. Materials are
metal, cloth, and clay.

Work in metal and cloth has the most
limited distribution partly due to differences
in technical traditions, and partly due to
problems of preservation. The south coast
of Peru provides an ideal climate for the
preservation of textiles and by a happy co-
incidence it was the locus of one of the
most spectacular weaving styles in the

world. Such a nice matching of environmental conditions and dominant technique does not always occur. With metalwork the problem was the conquerors' greed for gold and not the environment. Still, enough gold survived in Colombia to establish that region as the home of mastercraftsmen in this material. Less well known, because it was only recently discovered and much of it is in private collections, is the Mochica metalwork from the site of Vicus in northern Peru, which Lapiner publishes on pages 148-164. Here technical ingenuity served the desire for dramatic visual effects. Pierced forms, dangles, inlays, gilding, and bimetalism were employed to represent an incredible variety of subjects ranging from a man grasping a trophy head to a spider on its web.

Although clay was not always a primary medium for the expression of sacred themes, it was used in every period and in every area. Ceramics provide one of the unifying themes of this book. Monumental in that they pertain to the tomb and are enduring reminders of religious concerns, the objects in clay reveal the ancient Americans' skill in painting and sculpture. In general the preference for painting or modeling seems to have geographic significance. Artists of the north coast of Peru preferred a plastic expression that reached its height in the Mochica culture, whereas painting predominated on the south coast. All of Peru, however, was concerned with elaborations of the vessel form and the transformation of pots is one of the great achievements of Peruvian art.

Illustrations in this book are arranged by subject matter so the main themes of ceramic imagery are established. A page of animal stirrup-spout vessels from the early Mochica culture (400 B.C.-A.D. 1) is deceptively straightforward. A mother sea lion clutching her pup under her flipper seems to document the whim of an artist but another sea lion pup is also illustrated, suggesting that the subject had some significance beyond its immediate appeal. Figurines were not common in Peru, with some important exceptions such as the compact Nazca lady (Fig. 479) or the pillowy female

from the Chancay culture (Fig. 673). In Ecuador a figurine tradition flourished, occasionally producing works of startling realism such as the torso of a man from La Tolita which appears as the frontispiece in this book.

The pages allotted to each area in the book reflect the amount of information and material available. Emphasis is on the best known cultures of Peru yet there are sections on Ecuador, Colombia, Venezuela, Bolivia, Argentina, Chile, and Brazil, and their inclusion calls attention to the fact that Peruvian art did not develop in isolation. Questions on the nature and extent of interregional contacts are discussed in the introductory texts; the art itself, however, is the best evidence of these contacts. Uniform art styles are exceptional in western South America; regional traditions, whether due to environmental factors as is often supposed, or to stylistic and technological preferences independent of climate, have always maintained themselves with impressive vigor, but this vigor is obviously nourished by selective and periodic influences from the outside. This book illustrates the cross-fertilization between cultures, sometimes contemporaneous and sometimes separated by significant amounts of time. (Obviously, grave looting was not limited to post-contact times.) As an art book, *Pre-Columbian Art of South America* does justice to the complexity, variety, and beauty of many of the artistic traditions of South America as we know them. ⬤

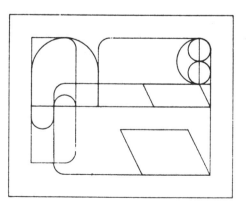

A Minority Report on the True Avant-Garde

Popular Artists of Brazil
By Selden Rodman
The Devin-Adair Company. $10.00.

SUSAN MANSO

In *Popular Artists of Brazil* Selden Rodman celebrates the kind of painting and sculpture that is variously known as primitive, naïve, folkloristic. No name is neutral enough anymore and describing this art, virtually unknown outside Brazil, one resorts to simile: it is like the primitive portraits, the landscapes and the carvings—from weathervanes to toys—that an earlier America produced; and it has affinities with much African sculpture or the folk icons that craftsmen of medieval Europe and the later baroque, especially in the European south, carved. In more recent time it is like, as Rodman says, the paintings of a Camille Bombois or a Horace Pippin. None of the similes can be precise. Whether secular or religious, all the art is representational, ranging from the anecdotal, almost purely decorative, to the emotionally wrought, almost purely private vision.

Rodman makes very large claims for this art about which he feels passionate. For myself, although I don't feel as strongly about all the work by the twenty-one artists he covers, I do very much like the spirit behind Rodman's celebration of it. His is a polemical spirit, attracted not only by the art but by what he believes it signifies. For Rodman, Brazilian popular art is "one of the major seedbeds of the counterculture," an art with its roots in the life of nature and man and not, a cash register; on the other hand, he sees most modern art—at least the art that sells—as disconnected from life, overly cerebral and fully corrupt. In a word, his chosen Brazilian artists—Djanira Nhó Ca-

SUSAN MANSO is a free-lance critic specializing in contemporary art.

boclo, José Antonio da Silva, Louco, Waldomiro de Deus, GTO and Júlio Martins da Silva, among them—are good (as were those primitives he earlier wrote about in his series of books about Haiti) and most modern —i.e., formalistic—art is bad. It is an argument whose spirit—as much political as esthetic—I can buy. *Artforum* would not.

Who knows, of course, if this particular handful of painters and sculptors who pocket the vast Brazilian landscape, most of whom are poor and ignored, a few wealthy, are really the new Giottos, the Byzantines of our time—these and other comparisons are made. One can't know from these photos (the color plates aside, rather poor) and even if, as Rodman has done, one had travelled the width and length of Brazil such pronouncements would be hard to make. The argument *is* inflated, a mirror image— down home style—of *Artforum's* incomprehensible electronic age jargon. But at least one knows why Rodman likes these painters and sculptors and more, one gets some notion of what they are actually, not philosophically, about.

Rodman describes these artists, including many women, in their studios, front porches and cafés. We learn where and how they live, and how much they earn. That Rodman paid fifty dollars for the Bahian sculptor Louco's wooden "Virgin With Penitent Angels," that Nhó Caboclo outwits his gallery dealer by taking one of his marvelous pieces (the stabiles, or "splits," partitioned off figures within a frame, and mobiles, moveable found-object assemblages) to the marketplace and selling it for a chicken or a bottle of distilled rum, or that the painter José Antonio da Silva proudly shows off his closet packed full of clothes and the deodorants on his dressing table . . . such are what we read about. It is family gossip and it works: this is the way an art critic who did not trust explication and felt strongly about an art connected to daily life should sound. Writing of the sculptor GTO's magnificent, intricately carved wheel of figures, Rodman's remark is characteristic. "In a way," he says, "it's absurd to do more than *enjoy* such art with the same open-minded reverence that went into its creation."

There is much to enjoy. Being escorted about Brazil and told how each artist lives, works and thinks—together with photos of the work and the artists themselves—makes for a modest book. Even if one isn't fully convinced that we are encountering genius in the backlands (and that is the book's subtitle), it is still true that unlike the current and usual run of art criticism, Rodman says something. Although he does not quote him, Rodman would agree with Ortega y Gasset: as art has moved from symbol to sign it has become dehumanized.

I'm glad that Rodman is around to both ferret out and talk about a different kind of art and that there are publishers such as his own small press to print what he has found. As simple as the argument gets at times, one feels we have never needed it more. I'd guess too that anyone who tells us that his much loved collection was bought for pennies is not out to sell it at a vast profit next week. If so, the criticism and the life are of a piece. That's nice too.

El arte ha demostrado ser más perdurable que guerras, escándalos, y crisis petroleras

—Osborn Elliott
Editor, Newsweek